The Eighteen-Year-Old Replacement

R. Richard Kingsbury

The Eighteen-Year-Old Replacement FACING COMBAT IN PATTON'S THIRD ARMY

University of Missouri Press   Columbia and London

Library of Congress Cataloging-in-Publication Data

Kingsbury, R. Richard (Roscoe Richard), 1926–
    The eighteen-year-old replacement : facing combat in Patton's
Third Army / R. Richard Kingsbury.
        p.   cm.
    Summary: "The WWII story of a midwestern teen who was drafted
six weeks after D-Day and sent to the Siegfried Line to fight in
General George Patton's 94th Infantry Division. Kingsbury reveals
what he endured both physically and emotionally – and tells how
he went from boyhood to manhood almost overnight"—Provided by
publisher.
    ISBN 978-0-8262-1781-3 (alk. paper)
  1. Kingsbury, R. Richard, 1926–   2. United States. Army. Infantry
Division, 94th.   3. World War, 1939–1945—Regimental histories—
United States.   4. World War, 1939–1945—Campaigns—Western Front.
5. World War, 1939–1945—Personal narratives, American. 6. Soldiers—
United States—Biography.   I. Title.
    D769.394th .K56 2008
    940.54'2143—dc22   2008001897

♾ This paper meets the requirements of the
American National Standard for Permanence of Paper
for Printed Library Materials, Z39.48, 1984.

Designer: Jennifer Cropp
Typesetter: BookComp, Inc.
Printer and binder: The Maple-Vail Book Manufacturing Group
Typefaces: Palatino, Adobe Garamond

*The University of Missouri Press offers its grateful acknowledgment to
an anonymous donor whose generous grant supports the publication
of outstanding scholarship.*

This book is dedicated to the eighteen-year-old
infantry replacements of World War II.

Preface

———————— This account is completely autobiographical and entirely factual within the limitation of memory, though written from the level of long-held images, vivid impressions, and feelings. I attempted to show the love of a boy and a girl and how it grew to maturity, the struggle for growth in religious faith, the struggle to separate childhood fantasies of war from the reality of war, and the struggle to relate to older men.

Above all, my main purpose was to show not just the events, but rather the feelings that were precipitated and conveyed by the events. I believe the emotions and their aftermath expressed in this writing are representative of those experienced by thousands of young infantrymen in World War II.

The *History of the 94th Infantry Division in World War II,* published in 1948, and the *History of the 376th Infantry Regiment between the Years of 1921–1945,* published in December 1945, were very useful in helping me to recall and describe the overall picture during the war.

I am indebted to the Library of Congress for information concerning eighteen-year-old replacements, found in the volume *U.S. Army in World War II — the Army Ground Forces: The Procurement and Training of Ground Combat Troops* by Palmer, Wiley and Keast.

Acknowledgments

First and foremost, I would give thanks to God for the inner strength and support over the three-decade-long attempt to properly present my story.

My wife, Mary Jo, was the love of my life and a source of overwhelming support during the war years, as she has continued to be through sixty-one years of marriage that have brought us two children, six grandchildren, and four great grandchildren. In my intermittent attempts during the last thirty years to attain publication, Mary Jo was both typist and chief spelling editor. Additional stars may be added to her crown because, by her own admission, she felt that our efforts to see my manuscript in print would be fruitless, judging from our experiences with publishers who seemed to want bigger-than-life–hero stories.

The love and support that my parents expressed in their letters to me is beyond measure. I'm sure that their fears and concerns were heightened by the fact that I was their only child. I was blessed to see my father live until he was almost eighty-six and my mother until she was ninety-four.

The technical side of getting the final manuscript ready for publication became a family affair, and we are deeply grateful to our daughter, Cheryl Long, for setting up our computer according to the required guidelines. Our oldest grandson, Rob Kingsbury, was a major player at a critical point in our computer illiteracy; he put the manuscript and illustrative material (pictures, maps, etc.) on the required disks. Words can't express our gratitude for his help.

Mary Jo and I both express our appreciation to our family physician, Dr. Cynthia Glass, who for so many years has kept us alive and well, enabling me to be around to write this book.

Though they never knew it, I have always considered Marjie and Jim Mordy along with Marvin and Diane Querry as godparents of the original story. In early 1977, we all sat at a Chinese restaurant, and they, along with Mary Jo, listened patiently as I told of some of my experiences as an eighteen-year-old replacement. I have listed Marjie first because of her saying, "You were just babies." Of course we were not babies, but we were young. I've often thought that her remark stemmed from a mother's love for her own son, then eighteen.

At the end of the dinner came the usual fortune cookies. I have absolutely no recollection of the message in mine. For sure, it wasn't "Write a Book"; however, after it twisted around in my mind for a few minutes, it evidently came out just that, because it was then and there that I decided to write of my experiences as an eighteen-year-old infantry rifleman replacement in Gen. George S. Patton's Third Army.

I want to thank E. Thomas McClanahan of the *Kansas City Star* for publishing my article about eighteen-year-old replacements and Jim Burns, editor of *Attack*, the quarterly publication of the Ninety-fourth Infantry Division Association, for reprinting the *Kansas City Star* article.

I am deeply indebted to Dr. James McKinley, who for many years was director of creative writing at the University of Missouri at Kansas City. In 2005, over a four-month period, he did a wonderful job of helping me revise my manuscript.

Many thanks also to Ben Furnish, editor of the UMKC Press, for his evaluation of the manuscript and for information on how to secure publication. Amy Lucas, with *New Letters Magazine* at the university, earned brownie points by typing up my initial manuscript with all its many handwritten inserts and additions.

I'm very appreciative of the encouragement and advice given to me by William A. Foley Jr., author of *Visions from a Foxhole*. We were in adjacent regiments of the Ninety-fourth Infantry Division.

Gary Kass was my acquisitions editor for the University of Missouri Press, and I could not ask for anyone more helpful, thoughtful, or friendly. Special gratitude goes to Sara Davis, assistant managing editor, who was assigned to smooth out the rough edges of a first-time author. Her painstaking attention to detail was exceeded only by her patience. Thanks, Sara!

Last but certainly not least, I give many thanks to Robert Ferrell, professor emeritus of Indiana University, for his many insightful suggestions.

Author's Note

This autobiography was written in 1977 with some revision in 2007.

I am the recipient of five separate 10 percent disability compensations from the Veterans Administration. Two relate to permanent damage to my legs due to my feet freezing during the Battle of the Bulge. Two are for loss of hearing due to concussion from German artillery in General Patton's breakthrough of the Large Siegfried Line on the east side of the Saar, also known as the German West Wall. The fifth one is for a German rifle wound to the right side of my chest, which I sustained during Patton's attack on Ludwigshafen on the west bank of the Rhine River.

I hold the Combat Infantry Badge, the Purple Heart Medal, and the Bronze Star Medal for meritorious service.

The Eighteen-Year-Old Replacement

Chapter One

As I look back now on the war, it seems like a *dream*. Not necessarily a bad dream, because it encompasses so many things, good and bad. All of it, including the tragedies, doubtless contributed to my maturity and later development. Nevertheless, there is an unreal quality about looking back on, and trying to identify with, an eighteen-year-old boy whose country asked him to be a man. It is only in moments of deep reflection that I can leave my present mindset, in which I neither express nor feel any deep hatred or fear of war, and slip back into the mind of that young man, who certainly experienced both.

It is only fitting, I suppose, to delve somewhat into the salient points of the years leading up to my eighteenth birthday. I was born April 10, 1926, in Kansas City, Kansas, and knighted with the regal name Roscoe Richard Kingsbury Jr. I considered it fortunate that I was referred to as Richard or Dick instead of Roscoe (the name used by my father) because when I was a boy the only other Roscoe I ever heard of was the actor Roscoe Karns, who wasn't exactly the hero type.

I was the only child of a middle-class couple who had a small business selling and repairing vacuum cleaners. When I was two and a half, we moved to Kansas City, Missouri. I was a Boy Scout, attended Central High School, and was Master Councilor of the Mother Chapter of DeMolay. Mother Chapter Alpha was the original chapter of DeMolay, a junior Masonic organization for boys that later spread worldwide.

Only children are often given to make-believe games, and I was constantly pretending to be a soldier. My father had been a drill sergeant in World War I, and I had pumped him dry on the order of ranks and the table of organization of all infantry units.

In my fantasies, I advanced quickly through the noncommissioned ranks to become a second lieutenant. Then leading my platoon to victory gained me a captaincy. I easily continued my climb, and by the time I next assembled my regiment for the charge, the eagles of a colonel were securely placed on my shoulders. Brigadier and major general soon followed, and finally I was forced to invent the rank of general general, which surely must be the ultimate.

Amazingly, I was never killed. Leading my troops over the ramparts instilled in me no fear. Though droves of my men fell around me, I always remained unscathed. To be sure, sometimes I would catch a stray bullet, and I would have to be carried to the rear, but this was only in order to have my head placed in the lap of a beautiful woman who would make a fuss over me.

I devoured old pre–World War I history books showing brilliantly colored maps of all the various countries. Consequently, my military victories were often those of a royal conqueror gobbling up one country after another. A few years ago my wife, Mary Jo, stumbled across one of these books and read to me the cover notations I had made as a child. I wrote, "I conquered Bulgaria, then Monte Negro, then Serbia," etc. and "now I am King of the World!" Since then, if I tend to be imperious upon occasion, her blue eyes sparkle, and she says, "OK, King of the World!"

The games of my childhood were not completely of the imaginary variety; I was part of a neighborhood gang whose leader was Bud Childers. We were not the only gang in the area by any means. Kermit Brown's gang was several blocks away. In some mysterious manner our envoys would meet and set up a battle, usually for a Saturday afternoon. The weapons would be agreed upon ahead of time. Sometimes it was wooden swords and garbage can lids for shields. At other times it was mud balls, occasionally with small rocks hidden inside. But the most exciting of all were the rubber gun wars. The week preceding a rubber gun battle was one of anticipation and preparation. A call for additional troops went out to the fringes of our neighborhood. Our fathers would make us wooden pistols or rifles with barrels fashioned out of broomsticks. Each one had a clothespin securely anchored to the butt end to receive a large rubber band stretched from the muzzle. The rubber bands were strips about half an inch wide cut from old automobile inner tubes. Sometimes two or three of these rubber bands would be tied together, depending on the length of the pistol or rifle. When the clothespin was squeezed, the rubber band was propelled in a somewhat wobbly trajectory in the general direction in which the gun was aimed.

The battleground was a huge mound of dirt known as Bunker Hill, which was in back of Altman's greenhouse, and the gangs would take turns being defenders or attackers. To defend was fun, but responding to the call of "Charge!" took on the momentousness of Pickett's Charge up the hill at Gettysburg. If the weapons were rubber guns, you were killed and eliminated when struck by a rubber band. This led to a great deal of bantering back and forth: "You're dead!" "You missed!" "You're dead!" "You missed!" I'm ashamed to admit it, because of the pain inflicted, but I found the best way was to shoot 'em right in the head, making difficult any claim of not being hit.

At Sanford B. Ladd Elementary School, the older boys would often divide into teams at recess to play softball on the asphalt playground. However, on occasion, since World War I was fewer than twenty years in the past, we would divide into teams of Americans and Germans. Then we would extend our arms into "wings" and chase each other, attempting to get on the tail of an enemy so that we could bring our hands together, squeeze the trigger, and yell "Rat-a-tat-tat, rat-a-tat-tat!"

During summer vacations, our neighborhood gang of five would seek various forms of entertainment. One was to go to a large secondhand bookstore on the nearby Brooklyn Avenue streetcar line. Inside were piles and piles of used books and pulp magazines. The only ones we were interested in were pulp fiction with world war–based short stories about things like airplane dogfights and bombing runs. After buying and reading your stack, you would swap around with the others. After you had swapped with everyone, you would return the stack in your possession for a partial refund. It was really quite an inexpensive form of entertainment, and to boys growing up in the Great Depression, this was very important.

My childhood expanded into youth with the usual growing pains. The neighborhood gang stuck together and spent four years in the Boy Scouts, from age twelve to sixteen. As a scout I had managed to achieve the rank of "Star" and was one merit badge short of "Life" for the longest time. That merit badge was "physical development." The required number of push-ups was always just beyond my reach, as I would lose interest in developing my muscles after a time and then would have to start all over. Shortly before my sixteenth birthday, toward the end of my junior year in high school, Ted and Bob Brown and I turned away from scouting to the International Order of DeMolay.

This was in the spring of 1942, and the war was devastating the ranks of DeMolay, as the older boys were going into the service. Frank S. Land, the founder, lived in Kansas City, and Alpha, the Mother Chapter of the world, was located in Ivanhoe Temple just two blocks north of my home. The lower age limit was hurriedly dropped from sixteen to fourteen to maintain membership. Through sheer good fortune and the fact that the older boys were being carried off by the call of their country, I enjoyed a meteoric rise to the office of Master Councilor at the age of seventeen, possessing even the coveted degree of Chevalier.

The officers wore tuxedoes to the weekly meetings—white jackets in the summer and black jackets the rest of the year. It was the white one, always worn with a dark maroon artificial boutonniere, that was my favorite. Before walking the two blocks to the temple, I'd stand in front of the mirror, and I'd admit to myself that I looked rather dashing with my dark brown eyes and hair with the big wave on top, set upon a one-hundred-forty-pound frame, five feet, six and a half inches tall. I always rounded up, claiming a height of five feet, seven inches, and the wave was the result of five years of hitting the top of my head at just the right angle with the edge of my hand, like the tail end of a karate chop.

As I'd walk up to the meeting with my friend and fellow officer Ted Brown, I couldn't help thinking that the world lay at my feet. I had twenty officers and five hundred members at my beck and call, at least theoretically. Being the Master Councilor of the Mother Chapter of the world, I would meet Shrine dignitaries who were coming to visit Dad Land at Union Station, hold installations at the Municipal Auditorium, and lead off the dancing in the grand ballrooms of downtown hotels. I wasn't exactly "King of the World," but I wasn't any lackey either! Pride goeth before the fall, however, as I would find out not long after my eighteenth birthday.

Backing up a bit, I'd like to get on the subject of girls. Prior to the age of sixteen, there wasn't too much dating for many boys, partly because they just hadn't gotten around to it yet and partly because they just weren't old enough to drive. The dates we had were usually in the form of going to a school dance and out for a hamburger afterward, and we rode in the backseat of an upperclassman's car. My first date was with an attractive brunette named Judy Rusk. I knew that I was supposed to kiss her goodnight, but I didn't. To this day I can't remember if it was because I didn't try or because she wouldn't let me! The strain of it all evidently obliterated the old memory bank.

During high school I developed many friendships. In addition to Ted Brown I ran around with Jim Benjamin, Dick Radford, Jim Gold, Paul Williams, Fred Stratemeir, Leland (Rex) Johnson, Jim Cochran, Johnny Modlin, and many others. Most of my friends were drawn from one or another of the literary societies in Central High School at the time, my own membership being in the Central Emerson Club. Four of these societies were male and five female. As I look back on it now, I realize that to some extent they formed a social aristocracy for those who belonged and an unfair caste system for those who didn't. However, since I was one of the "ins," I enjoyed it to the fullest.

There were not many fistfights in high school, but that did not mean that physical prowess was not respected. There was one period when Rex Johnson and I would carry a roll of dimes with us if we were going somewhere such as downtown on a bus to a movie. He was tall, strong, agile, and a good boxer, and on one occasion flattened an obnoxious fellow with one blow. To me the roll of dimes only gave me a sense of false power, as I had never been in a fight and never intended to be in one. Besides, with Rex along who'd ever need to?

Having turned sixteen in April of 1942, I got my driver's license and started driving the family car. The war had brought with it gas rationing and the coupon book. "A" coupons only provided something like three gallons a week, but the Kingsbury Company truck rated "C" coupons, which were worth considerably more, and some of those coupons mysteriously found their way into my possession. With a mechanical steed at my disposal I started dating with a passion. There was some status to be gained from seeing how many of the best-known girls you could date. Strange as it may seem by later standards, necking was just about as far as anyone ever went with any of the girls. In a very real sense, necking provided almost complete satisfaction in itself. Girls who "went all the way" were rarely heard of and were not in the regular social swirl. To even reach the goal of necking might take a lengthy campaign. One girl I dated was a very attractive, vivacious bundle of energy, who would willingly get into the backseat and reward me with a single kiss after what seemed like an hour of wrestling. After a few rounds of this I gave her up, feeling the compensation received did not match the effort expended.

It was at a yearbook-signing party that I officially met the girl I would later marry. Central High School was a large school, and I had seen her at a distance in the company of some of the members of her literary society, the Aristonians. Walking home one day past the Eagle's Nest, a bookstore and confectionery across from school, I saw her standing in front of the store window. She didn't notice me, but I noticed her! Though it was one-sided, the chemical reaction set my heart fluttering until I could feel the pulse hammering in my throat. She was five feet, two inches and had long golden hair, a beautiful, sweet face, and big blue eyes. Her nose was softly rounded on the end, and her full lips were emphasized by the stylish red lipstick that she wore. The dip in the center of her upper lip was like the top half of a tiny Valentine heart. At the drop of a hat her lips would curve into a warm smile that flooded the world with sunshine. From her neck down, although she was only fourteen and a half years old, she was amply endowed, with all the right curves in all the right places. Her forearms tapered into unusually small childlike hands, while the curvaceous calves of her legs led the eye down to trim ankles and dainty feet. She was beautiful from head to toe, although I confess that at this stage of the game I may have viewed her in reverse order, passing quickly over the saddle shoes and bobby socks.

The signing party was a short time later, right before the closing of school in early June 1942. It was held at an Aristonian's house. Kids came in droves, piling in and out with their school yearbooks, swapping signatures and the usual trite handwritten notes all over every page and picture. It was there that I saw Mary Jo, and I wasted no time introducing myself. After fifteen minutes of chatting we wrote in each other's yearbooks. My note was somewhat unimaginative: "Dear Mary Jo: I haven't known you long (all of fifteen minutes) but it doesn't take long to see that you're a cute, sweet, charming girl. I'm really looking forward to being in some of your classes next year. Best wishes to a swell girl, Dick Kingsbury."

Her note to me had a little more substance. (Violet was the color of her Aristonian club.)

"Dear Richard: Well, I've only known you for about fifteen minutes—but I've been hearing about you for weeks from Fenimore and all the other Emersons I know—so I feel like an old friend. Here's hoping I get to know you better next year and find out if you're the swell guy they all say you are. 'One of those Violets' (Shrinking Violets—ha!) Mary Jo Mason."

After that, Mary Jo and I dated frequently until her father's death in March of 1943. We went to movies, bowling, and DeMolay dances, but we did not go steady. Bells had never ceased to ring for me since the day I spotted her at the Eagle's Nest, but that wasn't true for her. Having found out from a mutual friend that I had planned to ask her to go steady, and not wanting to hurt me, she headed me off at the pass by casually saying, "I never ever want to go steady." Outwardly calm, I said, "Me neither." However, after taking her home I was so upset that I walked most of the way to my home in a daze before remembering that I had driven the car, and I had to walk back to her house to get it. From June of 1942 until March of 1943 she hadn't let me kiss her even once! But I wasn't the only one! She had started dating her whole sophomore year before I knew her, and by now her nickname with a number of boys was "Holy Jo"! She was the type who had many friends, both male and female, and some boys also saw her as a counselor who could advise them on their rocky romances with other girls. Her refusal to kiss me, however, never dampened my ardor, and on Valentine's Day I gave her a box of candy. As of this writing, sixty-five consecutive boxes have followed.

Tragedy then struck suddenly: Mary Jo's father died on a Friday; on Sunday, Mary Jo, her mother, and her younger brother, Johnny, moved from Kansas City to Louisville, Kentucky, which had been their home until three years before. They were to stay with Mary Jo's older sister, Anne, and Anne's husband, George, who was leaving soon for the army.

Several weeks later on March 20, I gathered the courage to send her the first of the one hundred thirty-four letters that I would write her over the course of the next three years. These we have saved, along with two hundred fifty letters from Mary Jo to me, eighty from my parents to me, and ninety from me to my parents, for a grand total of five hundred fifty-four!

In my March 20 letter I wrote "—All kidding aside, Jo, I've missed you so much I don't know what to do. I especially miss those great big beautiful blue eyes of yours, along with that gorgeous smile, that chuckling laugh, and those cute little hands. I even miss all those many days you've ignored and snubbed me and made feel like a fool for feeling about you the way I did. I haven't had a date since my last date with you as I just don't seem to give a 'hoot' about any girl.—I'd like to say, Jo, that you have one of the largest and swellest bunch of friends that any one person is privileged to have. All the girls and fellows over at school were saddened by your leaving. They asked about you and expressed their regrets at not getting to say goodbye. Biser particularly wanted me to say 'hello' for him. He's a good boy, even if he is a Franklin.—I was interrupted in the middle of the last paragraph by Brown and Johnson who stopped in. We all went to Modlin's where there was an Emerson poker party. About twenty of us showed up and we had one of the hottest poker games in Emerson history. Believe it or not I won 90 cents." I signed off with a phrase Mary Jo had once used to describe me—"Your friend and true pal, Dick."

Billiwick's at Thirty-fifth and Prospect, with its hamburgers, barbecued sandwiches, and various soft drinks, was a popular hangout for the high school kids. It was owned and run by Bill Stamp, a stocky World War I veteran who had served with the British army in the Near East. There was never a person who was warmer, friendlier, or more loved by young people than was Bill Stamp.

In an answer to my letter, Mary Jo wrote on March 25 that she had been getting two to four letters a day from her friends. She also wrote, "I miss Billiwick's so. It was so grand that sometimes I could die or something when I think that I might not ever get to go there again. I miss you, too, Dickie. I know it's a little late to say 'I'm sorry' for the ignoring that you mentioned, but at the time I thought it was right. (In our last two dates I realized how wrong I was, and I really let myself go and had really grand times. I wasn't just saying that when I told you on our last date that I had more fun with you than I'd ever had before. I meant it.)—"

It was now toward the end of my senior year, and I think the saddest thing for me was to leave the Emerson Club. I had been the fourth-term president, and at the last meeting we elected the new president for the first term of the next year. In my May 27 letter to Mary Jo I remarked, "I imagine you've heard that Ed Fenimore got first term in Emerson. Isn't that swell! The meetings for seniors are over and I feel like I've lost one of my best friends—Emerson. I remember my sophomore and junior years when the seniors walked out for the last time and we stayed in to plan Senior Farewell. Well, last week it was my turn to walk out. It happened that when I got in the hall I recalled leaving my books inside. I got my books but was cheerfully informed that seniors were not allowed. I didn't get the feeling that I wasn't wanted, but the sad feeling that my time was past and I was no longer a real part of Emerson. I know that 'Strat' and some of the others who have worked faithfully since 'sophies' feel the same way."

Mary Jo worked in a dress shop for two months that summer then was able to return to Kansas City for three weeks in August because all her friends chipped in and sent her the money for a round-trip train ticket. She stayed with friends, spending half the days at Louise Springer's and the other half at Dot Pemberton's, but the evenings belonged to me! This time she let me kiss her; the world had turned around and I was happy!

Chapter Two

Over the next year, Mary Jo and I maintained constant correspondence. She attended her senior year in a Louisville high school
while I finished three quarters of a year in junior college in Kansas City.
I plied her somewhat with presents, such as an amethyst ring for her
sixteenth birthday on November 1. Her real birthstone was topaz, but
I didn't like the color.

On Valentine's Day, 1944, I sent her a large box of candy, which, as
it turned out, enabled her to send me a telegram. Because of the war,
all greetings and felicitations sent by Western Union were taboo. Before receiving the candy she had been trying all evening to send me a
telegram of Valentine greetings. She and the girl at Western Union
went round and round. Mary Jo would try a sentence, and the clerk
would say "Nope." Finally the girl told her, "Well, you keep thinking
them up, and I'll tell you if they're OK or not." Sentiments that didn't
meet with her approval included "So sorry that I can't be with you tomorrow" and "Valentine greetings to the grandest person I know," but
the candy's arrival provided an acceptable subject on which to dis-
course, and the telegram came through reading "Package received.
Thanks. Am thrilled to death but I don't deserve it. Letter follows.
Love—Mary Jo."

By now the pace of the war was accelerating, and those of my group
who were approaching our eighteenth birthday were particularly
aware of the implications. We had seen all of the flag-waving in the
John Wayne movies and gotten caught up in the excitement, but when

the show was over, you didn't have to be too bright to experience genuine fear of being maimed or killed.

A few of the football-hero types joined the marines, but the vast majority of volunteers tried to get into the navy, air force, or any program that would keep them out of the infantry. I knew of no draft evaders, but if you could get classified 4-F or limited service, more power to you.

In my sophomore year I had taken and excelled in ROTC. However, the following summer I spent sixty days in bed with Rocky Mountain spotted fever, and after that I was unable to take ROTC or gym class because of the risk of heart trouble.

My father well knew the dangers of the infantry, and he encouraged me to quit school at the end of March in order to take eye training and exercises from my optometrist, Dr. Ralph E. Littlefield. Improving a myopic's 20/200 vision to the 20/20 necessary to get into the V-12 officer training and college program was a tall order for anyone, but Littlefield made a Herculean effort. In addition, I swallowed dozens of vitamin A pills and quarts of carrot juice and gave in to my father's bright idea of walking instead of driving the six miles to Littlefield's. Though I was able to temporarily bring my vision to 20/60, nature was not to be thwarted, and I became draft bait waiting to be called up for induction.

In late June, Mary Jo and her family invited me to come to Louisville for a week. I accepted and spent the week as a houseguest sleeping with Mary Jo's brother, Johnny—big thrill!

I spent July waiting for the ax to fall. Most of my friends were in the same boat, displaying bravado and throwing farewell poker and drinking parties. Ted Brown's folks were very good about this until the night we diverted our minds from poker, jumped on one of the players, left him devoid of even a stitch of clothing, threw him out of the house, and locked all the doors. Then we grabbed three flashlights and decided to make him the star of the evening. However, he didn't seem to like being in the limelight so he kept running around the house, yelling "Let me in, you can't do this to me." After about five minutes we tired of chasing after him and let him back in. The neighbors hadn't appreciated our raising the roof two or three times a week, but this was too much. The next morning Mrs. Brown was informed by four families that she had better not allow any more parties at her house unless she wanted police interference. That ended the parties at Brown's house; undaunted, we merely shifted over to Doug Millikan's house. Underneath all of the festivities, however, in private conversation you could pick up the gnawing fears that were held by all.

On August 10, jokingly I wrote Mary Jo, "A week ago Monday I got my second letter from the President. The dear old fella wanted me to report to Fort Leavenworth this coming Monday. I called the White House by long distance and told him thanks for offering me a position in his armed forces, but that I would prefer not to take it. However, he insisted, saying that he needed me to speed up the ending of the war. Seeing it was my patriotic duty to offer my genius in behalf of my country, I decided to change my mind and told the President that I would be honored to accept his proposition."

What I didn't tell her was that when I got the letter my mother cried awhile and then said, "You raise a child all his life, and now they are going to take him away!" I had the same sickening feeling in my stomach that I had a few days before when I came home and they told me my cat, Inky, had been run over by a truck. Mittens, the pet of my early childhood, had been gone a long time, and for the last ten years this beautiful solid black cat had been very close to me. Inky was also dearly loved by my cousin Ellen Alice, who had lived with us for five years since the death of her parents. She had picked Inky up by the curb, still living, and taken him to a veterinarian. Despite the effort, Inky died. By the time I walked in the door Ellen Alice was crying profusely and my mother had tears in her eyes. Under ordinary circumstances I would have become part of the mourning, but I cried out, "With all our men in Europe dying like flies, here you are bawling over a cat!" Though I had a concern for the men overseas, my outburst was prompted more by an ever-increasing preoccupation with my own impending doom.

On August 15, 1944, I was inducted into the army at Ft. Leavenworth, Kansas, with the enormous pay of fifty dollars a month. This was merely a receiving center where you would stay for a week or two before being sent to some camp for basic training. We did little except some drilling and marching, old-hat stuff for me as I had taken ROTC.

Though I was later to have army buddies from various ethnic groups and all walks of life, at this stage my experience was rather limited. It was from this bias, as well as from an attempt to play the part of a citified sophisticate to my girl, that I wrote Mary Jo about my first eight days at Ft. Leavenworth. "At the moment I'm sitting Indian fashion on my bunk, with only half an hour before lights out. I'm still at Leavenworth but I won't be tomorrow as my shipping orders came through today. The barracks I'm now in is plumb full of 'squares.' About half of them are farmers and the other half are Mexicans (they look like Japs to me). There's a 'hick' over in the corner now, yodeling to beat the band. About three sentences back one of them came over and showed me pictures of his farm, chickens, and homely wife. It's a great life if you don't weaken."

Mary Jo gently chided me for my callous attitude by writing "It seems so odd to think of you as one of the ranks, a khaki-clad lad, and all that sort of stuff. You, who only felt at home in a zoot suit! From your letter I could tell you hadn't been too impressed with your comrades in arms at Leavenworth. That 'hick' you spoke of who showed you the pictures must have been about ten times as homesick as you'll ever be. I'm glad for your sake that you are happy-go-lucky. You'll probably get a few laughs, anyway—when you're not too tired from the marching!"

I was soon to get as homesick as the next guy and maybe more. The zoot suits referred to were a batch of padded-shouldered coats together with high-waisted pants which had baggy knees, tight ankles, and broad suspenders. They had been bequeathed to me by my older cousin, Riley Walter, when he went in service. I shared these on occasion with other Emersons who wanted to look "sharp." Looking in a mirror at my khaki uniform I could only think "How the mighty hath fallen!"

As it turned out, it was at Ft. Leavenworth that I received one of the two bits of favoritism that were directed my way while I was in the army. The head medical officer at the post, Colonel Strickler, who was in the same gun club as my father, arranged for me to have a weekend pass to Kansas City.

While there I heard some very sad and shocking news. I wrote Jo later, "As soon as I arrived home Saturday afternoon I learned that Bill Stamp died only several hours before. A small fire had started in the back of his place about noon and he put it out, but I guess the excitement was too much for his heart. The doctor told him to rest after his last illness but he went right on working every day and got only three or four hours sleep every night. His funeral was yesterday but I couldn't get there. All the gang chipped in a buck each. As yet I don't know exactly what was purchased with the money. There's going to be such a lot of fellas and gals who will miss that swell ole guy. It's things like this that bring us face to face with reality."

"Reality" was difficult to face because I knew that there was no longer any centralized location for the gang to return to after the war with Billiwick's and Bill Stamp now gone. I had the feeling of a navy flier who sallies forth from his aircraft carrier in mid-ocean, only to return later, almost out of gas, and find the carrier pitched at an angle, sinking to the bottom.

We left Ft. Leavenworth on August 23 on the most broken-down old troop train imaginable. We traveled a course as crooked as a dog's hind leg and were never told our destination until we arrived there. Having a seat by the window I was held spellbound by the clickety-clack of the rails and the steady passing of the telephone poles, which threw me into sort of a trance in which I would wonder what the future held in store for me. My thoughts went back a few weeks to when I was working in my father's vacuum cleaner repair shop and Johnny Modlin stopped by in his uniform to say hello. He had a furlough from his army training and told of exciting things like half-tracks, personnel carriers, and mounted machine guns that could mow 'em down right and left. But then he grew serious and said, "It's the memory of the good things like home, friends, and your loved ones that enable you to make it through the training and maneuvers."

I could see in my mind the short concrete sidewalk I had put in a month ago, that led away from the back double doors of the shop. I had written with my finger in the first square "R R K Jr—7–23-44." If I never came back, maybe this would be kind of a grave marker for me down through the ages.

At two o'clock on August 24, I noticed a sign and realized with surprise that we were in a section of Louisville, Kentucky. Later, in a letter, I asked Mary Jo if her heart had skipped a beat that afternoon as her "old friend and true pal" was probably not more than several miles from her.

We finally arrived in Ft. McClellan, Alabama, some sixty miles due east of Birmingham. It was reputed to be the second roughest IRTC (Infantry Replacement Training Center) in the nation, Texas being the worst. On September 5, I wrote Jo, "I'm in the *Infantry*. A rifleman at that. Of all the things I wanted least to be was an Infantry rifleman. This isn't just a temporary classification either. Hell and high water can't get me out of the Infantry after my basic training. Our officers have guaranteed us that we will be overseas in less than a month after our seventeen weeks' training. Well, that's life. I hope those Japanese women aren't as gruesome as their husbands."

The war movies had pictured the Jap soldiers in a most unsavory manner, and at this time it was the natural assumption that we would be fighting the Japanese after basic training, since things would surely wrap up soon in Europe following the recent successful D-Day landing in France.

Ft. McClellan was located in a barren valley surrounded by large hills, hills, and more hills, which were perfect for hiking. We spent the late summer in them covered in red dust and broiling in the one hundred degree–days. Despite the fact that we would each take a half dozen salt tablets every day to keep from having heat exhaustion, there were several in my company who passed out during training.

During the first two weeks we had many sessions on first aid, military courtesy, care and cleaning of our rifles, combat intelligence, chemical warfare, use of gas masks, map reading and tossing of hand grenades. Grenades were those nice little creatures guaranteed to blow you apart at thirty yards.

My second, and last, bit of favoritism in the army was received from my platoon sergeant, a veteran of the Italian campaign. He was also a Demolay Chevalier, and he noticed the large silver Chevalier ring on my finger. Partly because of this I was made platoon guide, second in command of fifty-four men. I think he was also influenced by my ROTC training and the fact that I was short. The platoon guide set the pace for all the drilling and hiking, and a long-legged pacesetter would have everybody running by the time the pace got to the rear ranks. At any rate he kept me off KP (Kitchen Police) duty, for which I was truly grateful.

My privileges, however, did not keep me from having to get up at five o'clock or having to do my own laundry for the first time. The washing of clothes was done by hand in a tub with a bar of brown soap the size of a brick. Seventeen of us lived in a chicken coop they called a hut. The food wasn't particularly good, there wasn't enough of it, and the only thing good to drink was water, and it wasn't cold. Once in awhile you had enough time to run up to the PX (Post Exchange). I wrote Mary Jo, "The only dames I ever see are the ones who run the PX and they are gruesome. However, they're getting prettier and prettier every day. (Could it be me?)"

The PX sold a foul beer with a name that projected a green image—something like "Green River" or "Pine Tree." It lived up to its name by looking green, tasting green, and causing you to turn green if you drank enough of it. Someone in our hut had a huge glass candy jar like you might see in a confectionery. This would be brought back from the PX filled with beer and passed around as we sat on our bunks with our feet tucked under our legs. This, of course, was the time for the ribald stories! I had engaged in my share of them in my high school days, but this was an altogether new ball game. In the past the boys had been merely repeating hearsay, but here were older men speaking from actual experience. Sessions of this sort with older men were the first of many that I sat in on during my army career. I usually just listened as it was quite educational and entertaining.

Back in Louisville, Mary Jo was working for the government, ODT (Office of Defense Transportation), at wages of one hundred forty-six dollars per month, and heavily involved in volunteer work. She wrote, "Saturday afternoon was my afternoon off at work, and it coincided perfectly with a Red Cross invitation to go to Ft. Knox to play the piano at the hospital there. It was raining cats and dogs, and so the sixty-mile round trip wasn't very cheerful. Now I've played the piano at every military hospital in and near Louisville. I don't get a large charge out of it, but the Red Cross says it helps the sick men, so I answer the call whenever I can." If she knew the tune, she could play it by ear, which helped a lot, since most of her time was spent answering the soldiers' requests for their favorite songs.

She also played the piano for USO shows. "Lately I have hardly even *seen* home. I'm working with a USO show for the first week in October, and part of it is helping a chorus of twenty voices get whipped into shape, so it takes all of my spare time. The rehearsal tonight is down at the YMCA and I think it is going to be slightly on the corny side, but don't tell anybody. The gals are trying hard, I guess, but some of them just don't have the talent they are so convinced they are just bubbling over with. Well, that's life."

By the middle of September, we were firing rifles. I explained to Mary Jo, "As I'm the platoon guide I was chosen as one of the coaches. The coaches go on the firing line first thing in the morning, then spend the rest of the day coaching the remainder of the company. We have to have our head about six inches from the barrel in order to see if the firer flinches. You can imagine what my ears are doing now—one's playing the Anvil Chorus and the other thinks it's an alarm clock trying to wake up a war worker. Besides that my shoulder feels like it has been through a meat grinder. However, this kid's a fair shot at that. That bull's eye really looks small at that five hundred yard range, believe you me. We fire for record next Saturday."

We did fire for record the next Saturday, and I made "Sharpshooter," ranking sixteenth out of a field of two hundred.

Mary Jo had asked about the latest fashions worn by the infantry. I answered, "Are you kidding? Have you ever seen an escaped criminal who's had to crawl through mud and barbed wire? That'll give you a rough idea how we usually look in our fatigues. However, in my class A's I think I look pretty sharp (of course I'm prejudiced). At any rate I did all right in Atlanta, Georgia, last weekend. It's a nice place but it's sorta far to go on a weekend pass—one hundred ten miles."

In several subsequent letters she asked me what I meant by "doing all right in Atlanta," but I never told her. It never hurts to keep them a trifle in suspense. Actually, I went to Atlanta to have the braces on my teeth adjusted. All through my school years I had somewhat of an overbite, as well as one tooth that went out farther than I wanted. After the time I was twelve, the depression being over and money now coming into the shop in a satisfactory manner, my father had on a number of occasions tried to get me to have my teeth straightened. Unfortunately, the imagined embarrassment of braces (properly known as "orthodontia appliances") was always stronger than my sensitivity about my teeth.

High school being over, and no social twirling at all going on at the hardworking junior college, I decided that now was the time to get the job done. So, at the rather late age of seventeen, I started with Doc Tansey, a wonderful old kindly gentleman who shot skeet with my dad. His method was a vast improvement over the common style of banding practically every tooth. The molars were banded; a single expanding stout wire was mounted along the outside of the upper teeth, straightening the front tooth; and small rubber bands were stretched from the eyeteeth to the lower molars to correct the overbite. Nevertheless, I didn't like to broadcast that I was wearing orthodontia appliances and usually reduced the broadness of my normal smile. The expanding wires were like a time bomb that had to be adjusted every several weeks to keep things from exploding. Doc Tansey had referred me to an orthodontist in Atlanta, and I was able to get two or three passes during basic training. Since I really didn't like to talk about it, I merely told Jo I was having a good time. It was great fun traveling on slow-moving trains that were so crowded you had to sit or sleep on the floor. And things weren't better in Atlanta, with the best accommodations for the night usually being a concrete floor in a USO carpeted with wall-to-wall servicemen. As I can only sleep on my side, a concrete bed wouldn't be so bad if they would just provide a small indentation for the hip bone.

I thought Kansas City weather was terrible until I arrived in Alabama. One minute it would be pouring down rain, and the next the sun would shine so hot the perspiration started streaming off your face. You'd clean everything up at night then go out and get it muddy the next day. I explained to Mary Jo, "We got up at 4:30 and marched to the rifle range while it was raining and through three or four inches of sloppy mud. We got there just as the sun was coming up. Our first position was a sitting one, so I had to park my rear end in a puddle of water and start firing. The powder blast blew so much water into my glasses I could hardly see the target. However, I was lucky and got practically all bull's eyes. No kidding, Jo, you would have given ten dollars to have seen me this morning. After I was through firing I had to coach. I was lying on my side in a pool of muddy water and sawdust with the rain streaming off my helmet onto my nose and with a cool breeze making me shiver from head to toe, when I thought of how downtrodden I must look. I started laughing like a fiend and an officer asked if I had gone nuts. This Infantry is really the life, I mean."

My mother and Mary Jo had just started to correspond with each other. I told Jo, "Do write her. She's a swell girl who's often been lonely because her thoughtless son was always too busy to think much about his mother. You spoke in your letter about not knowing me. I'm afraid my mother feels the same way and it is my own fault. Confiding in her is something I have seldom done. If in any way, Jo, you could make up for some of the lack of attention I have shown her, I'd be indebted to you for the rest of my life. I could never have written this a month ago but that was a month ago."

By the first of October, my group had changed companies with a different cadre of officers and noncoms for more advanced training. Without my Chevalier platoon sergeant's aid, I was no longer a platoon guide and was just one of the boys doing KP and every other detail that came along. I had received my last bit of favoritism.

The mess hall for this company was quite unique. Instead of the usual cafeteria-type service, everyone sat down at tables for family-style dining. This seemed like a pleasant arrangement the first time I observed it, with large bowls of food placed on the table. I had gotten separated from my friends and was sitting with old-timers only, who were well versed in the system. All remained deathly silent and tense until the mess sergeant blew his whistle. At this signal everyone grabbed a bowl he had been eyeing, served himself and traded off with someone else. Everyone except me, that is. Having nothing to trade off, I went the entire meal without a single bite and had to go get something from the PX to keep body and soul together. Needless to say, the next meal found me with my eyes on a bowl of potatoes and my hands poised for the attack at the sound of the whistle.

The training started to get rougher: we learned how to booby-trap an area and how to dig foxholes so that tanks could roll right over us. They had to be six feet deep and two by three and a half feet across. Every time a tank went over your foxhole about fifty pounds of dirt came rolling in.

I wrote Jo, "Thursday night was the big night. We went out on five man reconnaissance patrols, and like fools they put me in charge of one. The night was blacker than Hades and we had to go through a thick forest. It had just rained so it was muddy to boot. My orders were to go four hundred ten yards on an azimuth of 343°, then two hundred ninety yards on an azimuth of 80°, then two hundred ninety yards on an azimuth of 85°, then four hundred yards on an azimuth of 203°. This was supposed to bring you right back where you started.

"If you think it's easy to go through a big forest at night, just try it. In the first place, you can hardly pace off your yardage because you have to make so many detours on account of bushes and trees. In the second place, all I had to sight on with my compass were silhouetted large trees that fell along my line of sight. Naturally, as we advanced along the silhouette would change, and I'd forget which tree I was sighted on. As if that wasn't bad enough, King (my pacer) suddenly disappeared from my left side into a six-foot foxhole. He started cussing and I started laughing even though this was a tactical patrol. After I dragged him out it seems he had forgotten how many paces we had gone. After a few minutes we arrived at what we figured was a very, very rough approximation of our first turning point.

"I then lay on the ground (the other fellows covering me up with a rain coat) and turned on my flashlight to change my compass to the new course. I asked the others if they knew how to set the darned thing but they had been sleeping in class too. I hastily concocted a theory as to how it should be done, and of course it wasn't long before we were in the middle of nowhere. No kidding, Jo, our company would make a lousy bunch of night fighters as half the patrols were in the same fix as we were. At midnight the officers felt sorry for us and started blowing whistles and shining flashlights from the top of the hill that was our starting point. We managed to get back with no further mishaps except I tripped on a root, fell over an embankment and lit on my face in the mud. King got sweet revenge by having a hearty laugh while I crawled out of the ditch. That's life!"

Our chief source of amusement in what little spare time we had was using the Ping-Pong table in the dayroom for the ancient game of galloping dominoes. In the crap games played by the Emersons I'd be lucky to win ninety cents, but here the stakes were considerably higher. I had a great run of luck for about two weeks and considered living on my winnings and donating my army salary to charity. Then the roof fell in, and I apprised Mary Jo of the situation: "This last week I've had the worst streak of luck the world has ever seen. Jo, I have too much pride to ask you for a dime to buy a cup of coffee—so just put some in a thermos bottle and send it that way. Seriously, Jo, I have learned my lesson (I hope) and twenty minutes ago I swore off crap shooting for the rest of my natural life. Be a pal and hold me to it, will ya?"

As the war continued to accelerate, news would come from home concerning school friends being killed in action. I wrote Jo: "Remember Sam Grimes? Mother sent me a clipping telling of his death in the battle of Tinian in the Pacific. I had known him a long time, having gone through grade school with him. It's things like this that bring the war very close to you."

The training intensified; we were averaging about sixteen hours a day. We studied and fired the 60mm mortar, fired the machine gun on the range, and fired the automatic rifle at field targets. One day when we were practicing tactics they chose me to be a German sniper. I piled into a camouflage suit and a Nazi helmet and climbed fifty feet up a tall tree. Besides nearly falling out of the tree, I fired so many shells the bore of my rifle looked like a carbon depot.

On November 19 we moved once again to another company for the final five weeks. The new company commander was a lieutenant who had served in both Africa and Italy, and was he tough. On the morning of his first inspection he looked at my face and said, "Why didn't you shave this morning?" I answered, "I only shave every third day, sir," which was more out of deference to my manhood than to necessity. He said, "From now on I want you to shave every morning, soldier." I naturally accommodated him by whacking off the little dab of peach fuzz when I first got up, though it seemed to be a complete waste of time.

These last five weeks included an eight-day bivouac in the mountains, a week back in camp, then the final two-week bivouac and maneuvers. The entire seventeen-week basic training program was a gradual toughening-up process, culminating in fifty-minute cross-country runs, sleeping out in slit trenches in the snow and rain, and hiking for ten miles at a crack through the hills with full field equipment. By the time you added up the weight of your clothing, combat boots, helmet liner and steel helmet, full field pack, trench shovel, rifle, cartridge belt with cartridges, canteen, and bayonet, you had a grand total of ninety to one hundred pounds.

And that rifle. It seemed to weigh a ton, especially on the long hikes. The big problem was that my shoulders sloped somewhat, besides being small. On those with square shoulders, the rifle strap hung securely, but in my case, the rifle was always falling off, so I had to either tilt the upper half of my body to the left, which wasn't practical, or constantly hook my right thumb under the strap and push it toward my neck.

Despite the rigors, and the fact that I was an unwilling participant, I'll have to admit that the IRTC did its job, and I was in better physical shape than I had ever been before or have been since. There was a spring in my step that came from pure physical power; I had the exhilarated feeling of the professional weight lifter who has just pumped iron. I vowed that I would keep up with physical training the rest of my life. Of course I didn't.

By this time the long-promised sample of Mary Jo's cooking had arrived in a package. I thought the cake and cookies were delicious, but they didn't last long as so did everyone else. Turnabout was fair play, however, as I had helped others demolish the contents of their packages. She also sent a sterling silver identification bracelet, which I deeply appreciated, but the greatest gift of all was her latest wallet-size picture taken at a photographer's studio. I had carried younger pictures of her, but this one looked so much more mature. It was *the* picture! She was so beautiful I had difficulty convincing some of my buddies that it wasn't a picture of a movie star. I carried all of my pictures in the snap-in section of my wallet, and now this one went to the head of the class. For the rest of my army career it was the picture I displayed whenever I was in a group of soldiers that got into "back home" talk. I could always count on it to bring out the oohs and aahs. Though previously I had always kissed one of her younger pictures good night, I now shifted this act of affection to the new one. How much it was to sustain me in the months ahead.

Basic training was now wrapping up with a crescendo. We crawled through the infiltration course under machine gun fire, and one man got the bayonet shot off his rifle. We dealt with numerous problems, one of which I described to Mary Jo: "We broke camp at three in the morning and made an eight mile march in the dark through deep mud and rain to arrive at the artillery problem. We were on a high hill overlooking a large valley and several more hills. One of the hills to our front was the objective. A battery of 105s located a half-mile to our rear started a saturation shelling of the hill. The shells passed right over the observation post at a height of not more than fifty feet. It was the first time I ever knew that at times you could actually see artillery shells in flight. They make a funny spluttering sound as they travel through space.

"When our company ran the problem, my heart was in my mouth during this part. You advance with dozens of machine guns and automatic rifles throwing a crossfire not far above your head. Large charges of TNT were going off everywhere to simulate enemy mortar fire. We formed our skirmish line about two hundred yards from the base of the enemy hill and started throwing some hot lead from our M-1 rifles. Then we began the grand assault, accompanied by a heavy barrage from the artillery. The idea is for the infantry to charge the enemy positions with the artillery shells keeping two hundred yards ahead of them. The enemy is supposed to be still dazed by the shell fire when you get to them. They figure the lives that are lost by our own artillery fire will be more than made up by the dazed condition of the enemy. Well, they weren't kidding about the lives that are lost, because one man in my platoon caught a flying piece of shrapnel in the head. He died instantly so I guess he never suffered.

"The march from the final bivouac back to the main camp was a nightmare. Through bad luck the last problem our company completed was the patrol and scouting course, which in itself involved about twenty-five miles of hiking. We then broke camp and started the long twenty-four mile march back home, making a consecutive total of almost fifty miles. A number of men broke down toward the last and had to be put on a truck. I thought I'd never make it because my feet were sore and cut from just the scouting problem. I managed to drag into home base, though it was a day or two before I could walk without limping."

While out in the field I received a letter from Mary Jo informing me of the death of a fine chap she used to date in Louisville. I had met him the previous summer when he came by after basic training, dressed in his uniform, to say good-bye to Mary Jo before going overseas. She kept up regular correspondence with him while he was fighting in France in the infantry, and his death was a severe shock. I had no time to answer the letter until returning to camp. I wrote, "I was very sorry to hear about Jim Wandell. It was coincidental that thirty minutes before I read your letter our company was told that the infantry losses in Europe have been so heavy all eighteen-year-olds will be shipped overseas immediately. They weren't kidding, because I got my orders to report to Ft. Meade after my basic. However, I get a 10-day delay en route to go home. I'll probably leave here a week from next Wednesday. I'll only be at Meade long enough to get processed, then nine chances out of ten I'll be shipped to Cherbourg, France. You see, being an infantry replacement is a lot different than being in a division. Divisions usually fool around a year or so before they see action, but we merely are put in a pool and replace frontline losses. It's a raw deal and I'm not at all pleased. I only hope I can keep the same spirit as Wandell. I guess he died for a cause that's bigger than us all."

Though I had described some of the events of the last several weeks to Mary Jo, there was one that I never mentioned to her or anyone else. It was weird and impossible, but it happened. It left the first of a number of deep emotional scars that I would suffer in the months ahead, wounds that would heal on the surface, mending to various degrees inside through the years but remaining with me to the grave.

It was one of the many firing problems to which our company was assigned. Our platoons split up to different hills, and we were all to fire at a centralized hill in the foreground, on which were located the imagined enemy. Prior to the problem we had received the usual orientation by our officers, and as I had done in the class on setting the compass, I was mentally asleep or was horsing around or snickering with the fellow next to me like a schoolkid. Our platoon took the hill on the right flank, and we moved along a ridge, spreading out and then flopping down on our stomachs into sort of grooves in the ground that flared out at an angle to the right. These grooves had been formed by countless companies before us who had run through the problem. I lit on a grass-covered contour and began firing from the prone position at the smaller hill before me. When hearing orders to fall back I arose, but out of the corner of my eye I happened to notice beyond a grassy mound to my right another groove that was bare of grass and was at a sharper angle to the right than that from which I had just been firing. It was one of those things you notice but think absolutely nothing about, merely filing it subconsciously away in your cranium.

Shortly after regrouping at the foot of the hill we heard a commotion with men gathering around an ambulance and lifting in a young soldier on a stretcher. We heard it was a young kid from another platoon. I knew him only by sight and name as there were around two hundred in our company. He apparently had been struck by a rifle bullet, and we later heard he had survived. After a couple of days we also received word that the higher-ups believed from the angle of incidence that the shot had been fired from our platoon.

There was no official investigation by officers, as accidents of this nature were not out of the ordinary by any means. When you played with fire there were plenty of near misses, and sometimes people would get hurt. In our platoon, we began our own probe into the accident and talked among ourselves about how this could have happened. I joined in with the spirit of a detective hot on the trail of a murderer. They discussed the fact that while our platoon occupied the right flank on the ridge, the victim's platoon held the center position on a smaller hill below us. And then something was said in description of the enemy hill that did not add up with my memory of it. A row of dominoes began to topple. The mental picture of the firing groove with the sharper angle to the right started flashing through my mind.

With deft questions I began to inquire into further descriptions of the enemy hill, until there was no doubt. The grassy contour I had lain in was not a firing groove. I had fired directly into our own position!

I have never read a murder mystery where the detective finds out that he is the murderer, but if there is such a one, I know how he feels. I was traumatized and didn't know how to handle it. I should have gone to the officers and admitted to having mentally slept through instruction and told them about the grassy contour in order to prevent another accident. I should have visited the wounded man in the hospital. But I didn't.

I had never been the brave type but never the overt coward type either. I had a strong sense of honor, and in the two years of driving a car I had programmed into my thinking never to be a hit-and-run but to stop and do whatever I could for anyone injured and to call the authorities. I had always taken my punishments like a man, whether from my father or from the school principal (such as on the day in sophomore biology when I took a cow's eye the size of a billiard ball covered with loose skin and stepped out into the hall in front of Virginia Emery, one of the school's most vivacious and extroverted personalities, who was passing by. She of all people should have seen the humor when I stuck my hand in her face, squeezing the beef skin and causing the eye to bulge out. Instead, she went into hysterics, started screaming, and fainted!). I was not programmed, however, for a situation in which a period of time had elapsed before I discovered my own guilt. Who would believe that I had not known it all along? I dropped out of all conversation and remember sitting with my back against a tree, shrinking within and feeling that all eyes were on me. Discussions of the accident continued for another day or so amid my ever-growing feelings of being a hunted man.

Vocal references to the accident finally subsided, but for me the aftermath had just begun. To retain my sanity I transferred some of my guilt to my rifle. Though I had loved and played with toy guns all through my childhood and enjoyed shooting a .22 rifle in my early teens, my rifle now became symbolic of death, violence, and pain. I hated it and didn't want to touch it, to hold it, or above all to fire it. Try as I might, I could not pull the trigger or squeeze off a shot during the remaining days of training. Cold sweat would break out on my forehead, and my hands would grow clammy trying to break through an invisible force that kept them from pulling the trigger. The remaining days were full of tactics for a mass operation, which enabled me to fake the firing of my rifle and go unnoticed.

It was only after the war, some two and a half years later, that I received a measure of peace in this matter. I was attending the University of Louisville for a short time, and Mary Jo and I had starting attending MRA (Moral Rearmament) meetings. Through the counseling of Stan and Libby Newhall, to whom I will be forever indebted, I finally wrote the commandant of Ft. McClellan, explaining the series of events and asking how I could locate the injured party. He turned my letter over to the base chaplain, who wrote me that he could find no hospital record of a man by that name being injured. As I look back on it, this seems odd, but perhaps he might have felt it best for me to let the whole thing drop there. In any case, I can only hope and pray that wherever he is, he has been able to have a normal life.

Having finished basic training I was now ready to fly back to Kansas City for ten days at home before going overseas. As I waited to board the plane, the irony of it struck me. Here I was, a fully trained infantry rifleman who couldn't fire a rifle!

Chapter Three

My original plan was to stop off at Louisville on the way home, but Von Runstedt's winter offensive in the Ardennes changed all that. My training had been cut short by a few days and my leave abbreviated because of the Battle of the Bulge. I had called Mary Jo to see if she could be a houseguest with us in Kansas City. Thankfully she could. She said she told her understanding boss at ODT that she had to leave immediately, jumped on a train, and sat on her suitcase all the way because of the crowded conditions. Then she spent three days with me and my parents before I had to leave on New Year's Day.

Our last night together was one I will never forget. My parents had retired, and Mary Jo and I sat on the living room couch listening to a record of "The Way You Look Tonight." It was very late when Mary Jo fell asleep with her head on my shoulder, and I drifted off not long after. Mother covered us with a blanket when she woke up early, and when we woke up the next morning, the record was still playing.

At the airport we all put up a brave front, and the good-byes were said. Seemingly there were hundreds of other young soldiers waiting to board a large number of army transports. I knew some of them from basic training, and we carried on with stupid bravado. They all were probably as sick with apprehension and tension as I was. Maybe it helped a bit as we yelled at one another things like "You'll be in the first wave," "No, I won't," with mental pictures of D-Day–type assault landings.

A week later Mary Jo wrote of her feelings concerning her three-day visit. "It is just like I told your mother in the letter I wrote Wednesday night—I miss you so much more now because I know you so much better. It's odd, isn't it, that I feel closer to you after three days than I had in two and a half years? But I do. You see, I had taken you for granted I guess. 'Good old Dick, my pal' and all that sort of thing. I just never had occasion to sit down and analyze how I would feel if I ever had to do without you. Then when you wrote that you were getting your overseas leave, I was frantic at the thought that I might not get to see you. I surprised myself. It just sorta knocked me for a loop. Me, being upset at not getting to see my 'old friend and true pal'—incidentally, let's forget that phrase. Anyway, the panic was there, regardless of how amazed I was to find it. That's why I didn't have to think it over when you asked me to come to Kansas City."

She didn't tell me until much later that the ODT had forbidden its employees to travel during the holidays, to give priority to servicemen on the buses and trains; so she didn't know until she got back to Louisville whether or not she still had a job. Fortunately she did.

New Year's Day, 1945, was cold and windy, with snow still on the ground. The weather inside the transport wasn't much of an improvement as there wasn't a bit of heat in the thing, and we almost froze. It had not been made for comfort (or even with any seats) like passenger planes, and they packed us in like sardines in the belly of the ship.

We arrived in Ft. Meade, Maryland, late the same day after several short stops. The next day we received all our new equipment, including our rifles. My feelings hadn't changed one iota toward my rifle. I hated it and wondered how I would ever be able to use it. Dividing us into large orientation groups, they explained, among other things, how our insurance would be handled in the event we were killed. This made my day. "In case you're killed . . . In case you're killed," kept ringing through my head. That night, being a private, I was awarded a detail of cleaning up the supply quarters. I always hated mopping floors, but I remember fantasizing that night that somehow I was picked to be a permanent cleanup man because of my good work and consequently was never ordered to go overseas.

On the third of January, in the bluest of moods, I wrote Mary Jo, "Hi, honey. I'd like to start off with some gay remark, but I'm afraid my sense of humor is slipping. I've received all my new equipment and made all the preparations to go over. I haven't received my shipping orders yet but I expect them in a day or two. Jo, Mother gave me a letter just before I left that I was to open later. I opened it an hour ago and I nearly broke down and cried. She'll probably undergo a thousand deaths while I only chance one. Write her if you find the time, will you?"

Still hoping against hope, I asked for a special examination of my eyes, feeling that with 20/200 vision I should have some assignment other than the infantry. Concerning this, I continued on in my January 3 letter: "Yesterday we had our overseas physical, if you want to call it a physical. They didn't even check my eyes so I went to the dispensary about it this morning. The Major there was good enough to inform me that unless you were blind you were good enough for the infantry. As this will probably be my last uncensored letter I don't mind saying that they should change the name of infantry to cannon fodder. It would convey more meaning."

From this moment forward to the end of the war I had deep feelings about being railroaded, whether I was on a plane, boat, train, truck, or on foot. I was on a conveyor belt relentlessly carrying me to the mouth of a great meat grinder. Regardless of my struggles to get off or move to the rear, I was helpless to stop its forward motion.

One characteristic of army life was that it was easy to make instant friends whenever you changed your location or your group membership. At Ft. Meade I hit it off with a young soldier whose name I believe was Hefner. He was from the Midwest, a little bigger and heavier than I, but also eighteen and just as unhappy about going overseas into combat. We had a strange relationship. We formed kind of a losers' club for two, commiserating with each other in morbid talk of how slim our chances were for coming out of the whole mess unscathed.

We continued our discussions for several days aboard ship, having left Boston Harbor on the erstwhile luxury liner *Ile de France.* Then one day an interesting phenomenon occurred. Hefner's personality seemed to have suddenly changed, and he would no longer talk on the same subjects, saying, "I'm just not going to worry about it anymore." Unconsciously I sensed what had happened to him, and his leadership enabled me to do likewise. The increasing agony of worry had finally become worse than any imagined horror of war could ever be, so you said, "To hell with it, what will be will be!" Fatalism is a stupid philosophy at best, but it is great for retaining your sanity.

There was little luxury left in the *Ile de France,* with the holds being converted to quarters for hundreds of bunks. Fortunately, it was a huge ship, and I was quartered in the middle, somewhat near the center of gravity, so I experienced very little motion sickness. In exploring the ship I found thousands of soldiers from all branches. One night, out of sheer luck I stumbled onto a high school friend, Dean Stringer, who was an armored infantry replacement. We went topside and stood by the rail with the outside of the ship in total darkness because of the danger of German submarines. We looked down at the water, where tiny lights, caused, I guess, by the phosphorus in the spray striking the side of the ship, broke the pitch blackness. We talked about the good old times in Kansas City. I talked about Mary Jo, and Dean talked about Ruthie, his young wife of one year.

I saw Dean a couple of weeks later near Le Havre, France, when we were moving from one replacement pool to another. It was for but a brief moment. I was in a truck going up a hill, and Dean was in a line of soldiers marching along the side of the road. I yelled, "Yea, Kansas City!" and the kid leaped a foot in the air in the old Stringer fashion. He'd always been one of the star jitterbug performers at our school mixers. Dean yelled, "Hi, Dick!" as our truck quickly pulled away. The memory of it has always made me laugh. Here I was, a foot soldier, riding in a truck, and there was Dean, an armored infantryman, climbing up a hill on foot. I heard later from home that he had been assigned to a different division than mine and was wounded. Other than these two brief encounters with Dean Stringer, I was never to see anyone during the war whom I had known before.

For fear of submarine attack our ship went to the north of England and landed in Glasgow, Scotland. Crowds of Scots welcomed us as we disembarked. I would have been more than happy to have taken a tour of the countryside and city, but Uncle Sam's idea of a tour was much different from mine. We immediately boarded a train and were taken at night down through England to Southampton. One of the conductors was quite friendly. He was English and had previously been in the English army at Dunkirk. He told us how the Germans thought they had the war all wrapped up and consequently were using dumdum bullets, with soft hollow points that went into a man small but came out the size of a fist. I remember thinking, "Thank God the Germans are losing the war. I hope they know it."

I never saw much of England, because it was night when we went through. Once in Southampton, we were confined to our immediate quarters for several days, after which the conveyor belt started to move again, and we were put on a ship to Le Havre.

On January 23, I again wrote Mary Jo, but my letters were getting shorter and spaced further apart and would remain so for the next two months until I was wounded. "Dear Jo, I'm sorry I didn't write you when I was in England but they rushed us so fast I hardly had time. I'm now in a replacement depot in France. What little I saw of England I enjoyed very much. So far all I've seen of France has been damaged by the war. It snowed last night but we had tents to sleep under. However, we slept on the ground. With the censor and all there's not much a fellow can write. Although I might add that I'm in splendid health (darn it).

"You know, Jo, it's only been three weeks yesterday since I've seen you, and I can hardly realize I'm here where I am. It's dark now and I'm sitting by a log fire. It's about to go out so I'd better get some sleep. I'll try to write you a long letter in a few days. I miss you very very much, Jo. Love, Dickie."

The censor had actually blacked out the words "replacement depot" in the first part of the letter, but he did a poor job, leaving enough sticking out that I can still clearly tell what I had written. The tents I spoke of were large, housing a number of men. I had made friends with two young soldiers my own age by the names of Kruger and Marrs. Marrs and I had the same first name, Roscoe, only I didn't like mine. An icy wind was blowing over the snow, and the tent didn't seem to slow it down much. We had yet to be issued our sleeping bags, so Marrs and I grabbed an army blanket and wrapped ourselves up in it as if we were in a cocoon. By cuddling together and combining our body heat we managed to keep from freezing.

Marrs, Kruger, and I stayed together through the replacement pools, finally being assigned to the same company. However, we were put in different platoons. Kruger made it through all the way into the Czechoslovakian occupation. Marrs was killed after only a few days on line.

A good deal of our movement between replacement pools was done by boxcar. They jammed us in. It was supposed to be forty men or eight horses, but I guess the ones who directed the loading couldn't count. There must be a better time of year or mode of travel for viewing the French countryside than looking out at the snow through the partly open door of a boxcar. At one point, however, things took on a bright hue when someone managed to snag some long loaves of French bread and bottles of cognac.

At one of the pools we were informed that we would be firing some weapons to keep loosened up. As I stood in line to take my turn I was petrified. I had been praying that I would be able to fire my rifle when necessary. At this moment there would be no conceivable way that I could fake it. When my turn came I raised my rifle to fire, but I couldn't. The sergeant yelled, "Fire that rifle, soldier!" I closed my eyes and jerked the trigger. The recoil that jarred my shoulder and head seemed to shatter the invisible glass bowl around me. After a moment I was able to empty the remaining seven cartridges in my clip, sending the bullets deep into the sandbag. I next fired a carbine and .45 pistol, and the ice was thoroughly broken, and though I still hated my rifle, I knew that I could fire it if the occasion arose.

The arrival at the Third Army replacement pool was momentous for all of us. Everybody had heard of "Old Blood and Guts," and now here we were going to be a part of Patton's Third Army! But I had more immediate concerns. By this time the wires on my teeth had expanded to the point that I would soon be in trouble if they weren't adjusted. I had gone to Doc Tansey right before leaving Kansas City and don't know what possessed me not to have my orthodontia appliances taken off. It was so hard to visualize what Europe would be like. I guess I thought I could go up to an officer and say, "Pardon me, sir, but my teeth are splitting at the seams because my orthodontia appliances need adjusting. Could you please direct me to the nearest orthodontist? . . . Paris, you say? . . . Yes, a five-day pass should take care of it nicely."

Well, I did take my problem to an officer, only he said, "I can't believe it! Soldier, you're not going to need those where you're going. Take them off." He directed me to where the dentist was located in a large old building. I have never decided whether he was a dentist or a dental assistant. He was young and frankly confided to me that he had never worked on orthodontia appliances. He convinced me that he was at least honest when he took a small hammer and chisel and proceeded to pound on the bands of metal that were cemented to my rear upper molars. His left arm had a vise grip around my head, holding the chisel against the bands while he delivered the hammer blows to the chisel with his right hand. I felt every blow down to the roots of my teeth, and I thought soon the whole works would be coming out.

All in all it was quite an ordeal, but he finally got the contraption off. As I look back on it now, maybe I set sort of a record. Though it was but for a short time, maybe I was the only soldier in Europe with braces on his teeth.

Chapter Four

By January 31 I had reached my final destination, which was a long way down the ladder. To be exact, I was a private in the second squad of the first platoon of Company E of the Second Battalion of the 376th Infantry Regiment of the Ninety-fourth Infantry Division of the XXth Corps of Patton's Third Army! At the moment the 376th Regiment was in Veckring, France, in division reserve, with the 301st and 302nd regiments on the front line.

The Ninety-fourth Infantry Division was one of only eighty-nine divisions that carried on ground warfare in all theaters of operations during World War II. Though it was strictly a wartime division, existing from September 1942 to February 1946, it had a brief but illustrious career under the able command of Maj. Gen. Harry J. Mahoney.

The division's first overseas assignment had been to contain the German forces trapped in and around the French ports of Lorient and Saint-Nazaire in the province of Brittany. Patton's army had bypassed these pockets earlier as it was considered too costly an operation to reduce them. From September through December 1944, the Ninety-fourth had successfully contained some 60,000 enemy troops, inflicting some 2,700 casualties upon them and taking 566 POWs. This was not accomplished without cost, as 100 men of the division gave up their lives and 618 more were wounded; however, it was from January 7 to March 25, 1945, on the western front, that it suffered the bulk of its 10,957 losses, of which I was one.

Division front, January 31, 1945

34

In early January the division had taken positions on the front line along a section known as the Siegfried Switch Line. This was a heavily fortified zone stretching for twelve miles between the Saar and the Moselle rivers. It was the base of an area called the Saar-Moselle triangle, the west leg being the Moselle River and the east leg the Saar. The fortifications were designed by the Germans to guard the approaches to Trier, a vital communications center some five miles northeast of the junction of the two rivers. The line was also sometimes called the Little Siegfried as it extended west at right angles to the main Siegfried line which ran along the east bank of the Saar. The main Siegfried line was also known as the Westwall, and General Eisenhower had long felt that the Siegfried Switch would have to be broken before any large-scale penetrations of the German Westwall could be made.

It was to this endeavor that the Ninety-fourth Division had committed itself from January 12 to the end of the month. Though its thrusts never involved more than a reinforced battalion at a time, they were continuous and at various points all along the line. The successes were measured in only thousands of yards of captured territory and small towns, but they represented a heavy dent in the German fortified zone. The Germans had contested every foot of real estate, and when it had become obvious to them that the regular fortress troops were not getting the job done, they threw the crack Eleventh Panzer Division, known as the Ghost Division, against the Ninety-fourth on January 18 in a series of vicious counterattacks. Nevertheless, the Ninety-fourth Division was able to hold onto most of the newly gained area.

Just prior to my joining Company E, the company had engaged in fierce fighting in the retaking of the small town of Nennig on January 23 and 24. The town had been lost on the 21st and 22nd, when the Eleventh Panzer counterattacked. The first platoon, which was to be my platoon, had knocked out three Mark IV German tanks, two by firing bazookas from rooftops and one with a rifle grenade, which hit the gas tank, setting it on fire. To stay clear of the machine gun fire that swept along the streets the platoon advanced from house to house by mouseholing through the walls. "Mouseholing" was accomplished by blasting holes with a bazooka rocket or with TNT. By the end of the first day the first platoon had captured eighty-eight prisoners and killed about one hundred of the defenders.

On January 26 and 27, Company E had advanced with the entire battalion about one-half mile to the Sinz-Bubingen Road. The first and

second platoons of Company E had made a costly attack across open
terrain to take several machine gun nests. It was at this point that three
German tanks appeared, and artillery was called to knock them out.
Unfortunately, a wrong adjustment was made, and the barrage, instead of landing on the tanks, landed on Company E and on Company
K of the 302nd, which had been attached. The barrage inflicted very
heavy casualties.

Later, on the north edge of Bannholz Woods, I was to experience the
feeling of receiving a batch of "incoming mail" from friend instead of
foe. The damage was nothing like that in the incident I have just described, but I wanted to scream out "Stop it! Stop it! You're shooting at
the wrong guys!" The artillery was a dear friend to the infantryman,
and many a rifleman owes his life to his supporting artillery, but once
in awhile somebody goofs as in all human action. Because of my own
nightmares through the years from either real or imagined wartime
guilts, I think my heart goes out most of all to the fellow who made the
wrong artillery adjustment or the bombardier who dropped his bombs
through error on the wrong area and later learned of the dire conse-
quences of his mistake.

At any rate, in the five-day period from January 23 through 27, Company E alone had lost 107 men, including every rifle platoon leader,
and it was in this setting that I joined them, at the last of the month, as
they rested in reserve in Veckring, France.

Before we arrived we knew there were about a hundred of us coming into Company E as replacements. I well knew the complement of
a rifle company was 187 men if they were in full strength, and 100 men
would represent close to 60 percent. It's impossible to describe the
sickening, sinking feeling you have when you discover this. I was
smart enough to know that the missing hundred hadn't been fur-
loughed to the States, and that old age, retirement, and problems of
longevity pay would not be topics of discussion.

This sickening feeling in the pit of my stomach was aptly summed
up by Stephen Ambrose in his book *Citizen Soldiers*. On page 278 he
writes about replacements who had been sent to my 94th Infantry Division. "In February, 1945, Capt. Douglas Smith, 94th Division, gathered a bunch of replacements in a cellar just behind the front lines. He
wanted to instill some confidence, so he told them they were joining
the finest combat outfit in the whole damned Army. After, he asked his
sergeant, Jim Morrison, 'Did I make sense, or did I sound like I was full

of shit?' 'You sounded sincere enough,' Morrison replied. 'But they know the only reason they're here is because someone else got hit or killed. Otherwise they wouldn't be here.'"

Looking back on it now, I can imagine the feelings of the original members of the company as they received their first large batch of replacements. In a matter of a few days they had lost more than one-half of the buddies they had been with and trained with for as long as two years and now were having the bulk of their ranks filled with green eighteen- and nineteen-year-old kids. As time went on, this became an ongoing process, with replacements replacing replacements in large batches about every two weeks. By the time I was wounded on March 23, there had been in the neighborhood of 250 additional casualties. There were three rifle squads of twelve men each to a platoon. It was as if everybody were lying on a giant roulette wheel with thirty-six slots, going around and around, each man waiting for a shell to fall on his number. The slots always remained the same. Only the faces changed.

Of course, on the bright side, if you could hang on long enough, the opportunities for advancement were excellent at all levels of rank, with the older men moving up to fill vacated job slots.

In addition to knowing that I was coming in with a hundred replacements, I was informed along with the rest that our opponent would be the Eleventh Panzer, better known as the Ghost Division. That's all I needed! I had never seen any real Germans and could refer only to the mental images derived from the menacing Nazi supermen I had seen in the movies. And now they were telling us about a Ghost Division.

As we pulled into Veckring by truck we noticed that the Second Battalion was billeted in what looked like an old army barracks. I was assigned to a room upstairs that had beds, and I had no sooner set down my equipment than the entire battalion of about eight hundred men was assembled outside in front of the buildings. I assumed we were going to receive some sort of welcoming address, but it didn't turn out that way. We waited, and before long a caravan of staff cars pulled up, and who got out but none other than Lt. Gen. George S. Patton Jr., "Old Blood and Guts" himself, flanked by a number of brigadier generals, colonels, and majors. It was the only time I ever saw him, but he was someone you wouldn't forget. He wore a helmet liner that shone like diamonds, probably because of ten coats of clear lacquer, studded with the three stars of a lieutenant general, and on his hips rode a pair of .45-caliber ivory-handled revolvers. He stood on something high to address the eight hundred men who were spread out over quite an area. There was no PA system, but he didn't need one. He must have had his own built-in amplifier, as I could clearly hear him at some distance.

I don't recall his entire message, but I assume he complimented the battalion for its accomplishments in the last several weeks. If he didn't, he should have. I also don't recall any welcoming to the newcomers, which is purely academic as far as I'm concerned; I would have interpreted it only as the warden's welcome to the condemned prisoner as he is about to enter the little room with the electric chair. What I vividly recall was the fact that he was extremely upset and agitated because some platoon somewhere had surrendered to the enemy. This, in his eyes, was a "no no," if you want to give it a gentle translation. The air turned somewhat blue with the choice words that he injected between shouts of "Never surrender!" and "Fire more ammunition!" I can't say that his address ever did me any good, but nonetheless it was quite a memorable experience to have seen such a colorful historical figure.

The real welcoming was done by the old members of the platoon, and there couldn't have been a nicer group of men. They were extremely friendly and took us under their collective wing. There were Ben Siegel, Vogel, and Chernak. Chernak was kind of a cutup and life of the party during those periods when the heat was off, and even when it wasn't, he could see the bright side and wear a smile. There were Moon Welling and Garnett Lee. I had not known Lee previously, but not only was he from Kansas City, he lived not far from me. He was twenty years my senior and the rough-and-ready type, having been with the fire department. Talking with him about the Forty-seventh and Prospect area, home didn't seem so far away.

Al Beardsley was the quiet, fatherly type who smoked a long, curved black pipe. He knew his business, though, as he was the one who had knocked out the tank with his rifle grenade. He probably was only in his thirties, but to an eighteen-year-old that was ancient.

Komisky was a bundle of energy and often flashed a big grin that had a way of cheering everybody up.

The leader of the platoon was 2d Lt. Nathaniel Isaacman, who was more enlisted man than officer. He had received a battlefield commission from the rank of tech sergeant right after the battle at Nenning, as well as a Silver Star. He was one of two who fired bazookas from the rooftops at Nenning, knocking out the Mark IV tanks. Ben Siegel had been right beside him handing out the rockets. The original members of the platoon called him "Ike," and standing well over six feet tall, stockily built, he presented a formidable appearance.

And above all there was Gus Graham, from South Carolina. Gus was six feet, six inches tall, slim and quiet, with a warm smile and a personality that could best be described as gentle, which might belie the fact that he had been something of a hero in the patrol activity around the Saint-Nazaire pocket. He was a crack shot with a rifle and had proved it there. I'd say he was in his late twenties, and if anyone produced a case of hero worship in me during the war, it was Gus Graham, not because of his battle achievement but because of his attitude. It was Gus who would talk to me during those first few days on the front line, telling me that if I just had faith in God everything would come out all right. Gus made it all the way through the war without a scratch, which is the way it should be for a guy like Gus.

Being in division reserve wasn't all rest by any means, as it is at times like this that the chicken details seem to take over again. There were formations, training schedules, and the cleaning of equipment. On one occasion the captain assembled the whole company to impress upon us the chain of command, which was obviously important in light of the devastating losses suffered in recent days. He stressed how every platoon and squad should ahead of time distinctly clarify who would automatically move up to fill any vacancies of authority, starting with assistant squad leader. Frankly, I didn't pay much attention; being a buck private, I figured by the time it got down to me there wouldn't be anyone left anyway, and I would be fully capable of ordering myself to do a complete about-face and advance to the rear.

It was during this period that there occurred a most unusual happening. We didn't know where, but somewhere in the higher echelons of authority, maybe in division, corps, or army headquarters, some lamebrain of a staff officer with shiny boots propped up on a desk, who felt he had to do something to be worth his salt, came up with what he thought was a brilliant idea. It involved the action of a special platoon on a night prior to an all-out regimental assault by the 376th Regiment against Bannholz Woods, which thus far had defied American possession.

All the platoon had to do was to blacken their faces, and when the pitch-black February night had settled in, proceed to cross an antipersonnel minefield that lay in front of Bannholz Woods. German Schu mines didn't usually kill you, but they had a nasty habit of blowing off feet. If the platoon encountered machine gun or rifle fire while in the minefield, they were to use marching fire from the hip with their rifles, partly to build up their own confidence. The survivors were then to infiltrate the woods in the pitch darkness, reconnoiter, and locate the enemy installations, compile a consolidated report as to their position and consistency, send a runner back through the minefield with the needed information, dig in for the night in the middle of the Germans, weather the massive artillery barrage that our ordnance would deliver at dawn, and then when the rest of the regiment began its frontal attack, fire at the Germans from within.

With twenty-seven rifle platoons in the regiment, guess which one they picked? First Platoon, Company E.

We listened to the plan in stunned disbelief. Danger was a soldier's lot, but particularly the part about gathering that kind of information in a woods in the pitch blackness was an impossibility that didn't *border* on being ludicrous, it *was* ludicrous.

To say the least, I was no tactician, but my experience in basic training with the five-man reconnaissance patrol and compass-reading problem in a pitch-black forest under a solid winter overcast sky had taught me the futility of much information gathering.

It's easy to fantasize about the whole operation: "After making it safely through the minefield, I started stumbling through the forest. Suddenly and without warning I fell in a large hole which turned out to be a German position. 'Pardon me, gentlemen, for dropping in this way,' I said. 'I'm just checking on your equipment. Is this a machine gun or mortar emplacement?'

"'A machine gun, you dumkopf!' was the reply.

"'Of course,' and vaguely seeing the faint outline of a massive contraption in from of me and wanting to appear wise, I followed up by asking, 'A heavy?'

"'Jahwohl!'

"'O.K., now let me get this down.' Taking out my penlight and notebook I carefully marked down one heavy machine gun. 'Thank you very much, gentlemen, I'll be stumbling along.'

"Leaving the emplacement and not having a compass with which to set an azimuth, I did a perfect left oblique, which put me on an exact course to the northwest. This had to be correct as we had entered the German lines going due north. Doing my best to maintain a straight line, some 313 trees and two gulleys later, I stumbled into another emplacement and repeated the previous procedure.

"At a prearranged time the platoon gathered to assimilate the information. The platoon runner held a kerosene lantern high over the lieutenant's head, and we all moved in close round him, sitting cross-legged on the ground like a bunch of Boy Scouts. 'All right,' he said. 'Let's take the machine guns first.' Quite a few of us raised our hands. He pointed at me, and I responded, 'One heavy machine gun eighty-five paces due north of the minefield.'

" 'All rightee,' he said, slipping a number of pieces of carbon paper between the sheets he had anchored to his large clipboard. 'One heavy machine gun,' and he jotted down its location. While I still had the floor, I piped up 'and directly northwest of there is a medium mortar at a distance of two gulleys and 313 trees.'

"'You said three hundred and how many trees?'

"'Thirteen, sir.' The lieutenant continued on with his tabulations, asking for light machine guns, light and heavy mortars, howitzers, 88s, and tanks, etc., taking care, of course to note whether the tanks were of the Mark IV or Tiger Royal variety.

"After he completed his tabulations the lieutenant seemed satisfied, then turned to me. 'Kingsbury,' he said, 'Since this is your first night on line, we'll give you your choice of returning the information across the minefield or staying here and getting the hell shelled out of you at dawn.' At first thought this appeared to be a choice of rotten apples, but as I got to thinking about it, I remembered that I had two lucky rabbit's feet, one in each pocket. Surely the one on the left would get me back. After I indicated my decision, the lieutenant tore off a copy and handed it to me, saying, 'You needn't worry, I have extra copies. If I hear a boom, I'll just send another.'

"'Thank you, sir. That's a comforting thought. I'd better be on my way.'

"Fortunately, the rabbit's foot on the left side did its job, I made it through the minefield, the information reached the proper authorities and everybody was happy." End of fantasy.

Whatever may have been my mental image of the operation, I don't think it varied too much from that of anyone else in the platoon. Since we had been given direct orders to carry out the mission there was no choice, ostensibly at least, but to prepare in the best way we could.

After verbal training sessions the time arrived for a dry run, which was to take place on top of the French Maginot Line. Veckring lay right at the foot of some of the large rolling hills that had been considered the impregnable defense of France until the Germans simply out-flanked it by going through the Ardennes Forest. Why the French hadn't extended the line to the ocean I'll never guess, but nonetheless, all through my youth I had read about the Maginot Line in the news-papers and had seen in the movies the intricate underground system, including railways. Upon my arrival in Veckring I had hoped to be able to take a tour of the fortification, but the only guided tours the army ever gave me were ones I didn't want to take.

On the night of the dry run the platoon blacked up our faces to blend well with the jet-black night, boarded trucks for the ride to the edge of the hills, jumped off the trucks, and away we went. I will never say that we screwed up intentionally, only that it worked out that way. As no one really had his heart in it, things fouled up from the first and then got worse. About that time someone started laughing. Then everyone started laughing, and the unspoken consensus of opinion was that as long as we were screwing it up, we might as well screw it up royally. With this in mind, a number of men started to stumble, with numer-ous rifle shots going off accidentally. It must be noted that when a rifle went off accidentally, it was always pointed up and away very conve-niently, so that no one was hurt.

The powers that be must have been listening and observing the fi-asco and realized the infeasibility of the whole affair, or maybe just the futility of trying to get anyone to do it. At any rate, we were soon no-tified that the mission had been scrapped, and we all breathed a sigh of relief.

Unfortunately, dumb ideas don't always die. Sometimes they hang around in diluted form. In a day or so we were told that the mission was reactivated, only in a modified fashion. This time just one rifle squad was to cross the minefield, find out whatever they could in the woods and then return. This made much more sense, though it was hardly something for which anyone would volunteer.

With three rifle squads in the platoon, guess which one was picked? The second squad!

On the morning of February 9, our squad of twelve men was put on a truck and sent to some house across the border into Germany, a short distance from the front line. We were told to blacken our faces and wait for our mission to begin after dark. To say I was worried and scared was putting it mildly, but by this time I was worried out. With a number of hours to sweat through, I took to rummaging around the house and found a German book on World War I filled with many pictures. In an ironic exercise in escapism I pored over photographs of German legions and piles of dead soldiers, both German and Belgian, as the Germans proceeded across the Belgian border. Just as fantasies of war had always gripped me as a child, so did they grip me during these few hours of waiting. As if it were a protective umbrella, my mind separated the fantasies of those few hours from the present reality.

Suddenly, an officer appeared at the door and said that the mission was canceled, and we were to return to Veckring. This news brought an outburst of tremendous joy to the squad, and we jumped around, shouting and slapping each other on the back. After we calmed down, we piled into a truck for the return trip to Veckring.

As it turned out, the regiment must have received orders to move up to the front right after we started on our journey to the rear. By late afternoon, on the road to Veckring, we ran into our regiment moving north. It's kind of a weird feeling to see your regiment moving to the front while you're moving to the rear, but we soon got the hang of it and entered into the spirit of the whole thing. We were proceeding strictly within legal lines. Our driver, probably from the transportation corps, had orders to take us to Veckring, France, and by golly that's what he was going to do! When we passed our company and the other squads in our platoon, we gave them the raspberry. They stared at us in amazement and wondered what was going on.

After the regiment had passed on, I recalled reading cases where soldiers had been stuck in odd places because of some mix-up in orders. Wild thoughts began floating through my brain about spending the war in Veckring due to the fact we never received orders to do otherwise.

However, the bubble was popped when we reported to some top sergeant, who immediately turned us "About-face!" and sent us back to the front. Later that night we rejoined the second battalion in the small town of Perl.

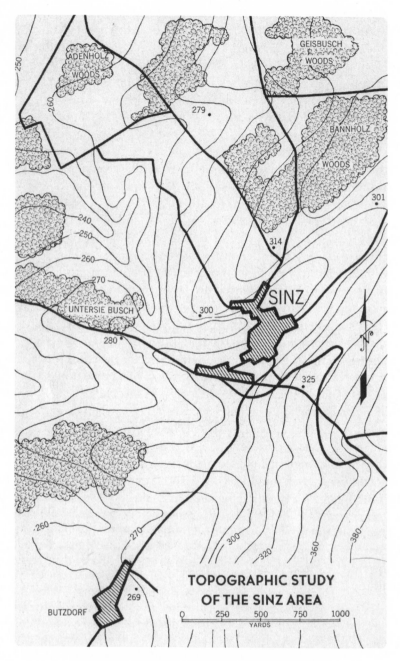

Topographic study of the Sinz area

Chapter Five

The short honeymoon for the 376th Regiment was over. The plan was for the Second Battalion to take Bannholz Woods on the morning of February 10, with the First and Third battalions then to pass through, turn east to attack, and seize Munzingen Ridge and the towns of Munzingen and Faha.

A few hours after our arrival in Perl, shortly after midnight, the Second Battalion again boarded trucks for the short trip to Nennig. At about one in the morning we left the trucks and moved northeast and then east in a long column along the Sinz-Bubingen Road until we assembled on the southern edge of a narrow but dense strip of pine woods known as Untersie Busch. The road at this point was the front line. It was so dark that squad leaders checking their men had to ask a man his name, even from a few feet away, to know who he was. The only sounds were whispers, the scratch of pebbles rolling under heavy feet, and the rustle and click of equipment being adjusted, sometimes to the accompaniment of under-the-breath curses.

Each rifle company was made up of three rifle platoons and a weapons platoon of light machine guns and mortars. The battalion consisted of three rifle companies, E, F, and G, and the heavy weapons company, Company H. The best luck I ever had, as it turned out, was that my company, Company E, was to be held in reserve in Untersie Busch, as the initial advance was to be made by F and G. Beyond Untersie Busch lay a draw some three hundred yards long down a gentle slope cluttered with dense and tangled undergrowth that offered

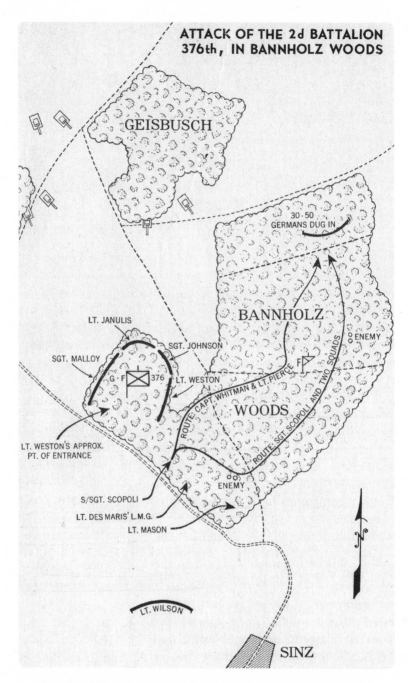

Attack of the Second Battalion, 376th, in Bannholz Woods

moderately good concealment followed by about six hundred or seven hundred yards of open ground at a slight upgrade that led into the dreaded pine forest of Bannholz Woods.

Bannholz Woods was an excellent place to defend. Situated high on the slope of a hill, its defenders could cover any possible routes of approach. Unlike many patches of dense forest, the woods concealed a mesh of roads that made it possible to maneuver tanks. On the east lay Munzingen Ridge, which provided a perfect observation point for the German artillery.

Shortly before dawn, F and G companies silently moved to the line of departure through a minefield that the engineers had cleared with their detectors and marked with paths. I presume this was the same minefield that our special night platoon was to have cleared by the "touch toe" method.

About fifteen minutes of our own artillery fire preceded the attack, which began just as it started to get light. Our supporting artillery continued as the two companies moved out, but nothing was heard from the Germans yet as it was still too dark for observation. The heavy machine gun platoons from Company H had been attached to the assault companies, along with additional bazooka teams drawn from the regimental antitank company. The bazooka teams were to handle the tanks that were known to infest Bannholz Woods.

Before the assault companies reached the woods it became light enough for the German artillery, and all hell broke loose. Most of the companies got to the woods, but their troubles were just beginning. Matters went from bad to worse to tragic. To recount the day's fighting would be a saga in itself. Under ordinary circumstances it would have been a high-cost operation but one with some chance of succeeding. Unfortunately, the Germans used this opportunity to display a new wrinkle.

The German Tiger tanks in the woods had been equipped with "bazooka skirts," each of which consisted of a thin outer sheet of metal plate guarding the vital spots on the hull. This outer skin was separated from the hull itself by an area of dead space. Bazooka rounds would penetrate the skirt and explode harmlessly on the hull without penetrating to the tank's interior. More than anything else, the inability of the bazooka teams to damage the German tanks led to our defeat that day.

The battle with the German infantry was nose to nose, with both sides sniping at each other from behind trees only a few yards apart. Prisoners were taken and then lost again as captors and the captured, both taking cover from the furious shelling of the tanks, lost one another in the confusion. The remnants of the American troops dug foxholes as morning turned to afternoon. The morning drizzle changed into a steady soaking rain that collected in yellow pools at the bottom of every foxhole and made a nightmare of quicksand of the churned-up ground where tanks had passed.

The German tank drivers gained confidence as the bazooka rockets proved harmless, and they began searching for individually occupied foxholes. A tank would move to within a few feet of a foxhole and blast away with its cannon. The battle now became a slaughter, and resistance began to crumble.

Back in Untersie Busch, Company E knew that things weren't going well in Bannholz Woods by the sound of constant shelling. We had contributed men for litter bearers earlier in the day, but accurate information was lacking, as the assault companies were spread out in Bannholz over separated areas.

It wasn't until late afternoon that our company was committed. As we moved out, we saw the results of previous days' artillery fire. There was a knocked-out German tank with a crewman lying close by, burned to a cinder. A group of German soldiers had evidently fed the cannon and lay piled where they had died. We eyed them without compassion as we passed by. These were the first Germans I had seen, and I stared at one large, blond-headed, stockily built corpse that fit the mental image I had of the German male. They appeared distorted to me—like logs, without animation. It was difficult to realize that they had once been living, breathing human beings.

Led by our battalion commander, Lt. Col. Martin, we advanced in spread formation down the gentle slope. The German artillery soon spotted us and began firing. At first the shells landed at a distance, and for one brief moment it was thrilling and exciting. I could see for quite a distance in all directions over the rolling hills and forests and felt akin to the infantry that used to advance in the Napoleonic wars. Once again I was at Bunker Hill in back of Altman's greenhouse, and my gang was preparing to attack Kermit Brown's gang with rubber guns. I remember thinking stupidly for a moment, "This isn't so bad!"

Then, with a shrill whistle followed by a deafening explosion, one hit close. The shrapnel roared by my ear, and with all my heart and soul I wanted to dive into a hole or at least hit the ground, but the rules said "keep going." The cold hard facts began to sink in. It wasn't like toy soldiers.

It's a funny feeling to know that someone wants you dead and is trying his best to kill you. There is no way basic training can prepare you for this feeling, as any fire thrown close to you in training is known to be from a friend. Thankfully, I've never had the experience of knowing that the Mafia had put out a contract on me, but if I had, I suspect that the feeling would be similar to the one I am attempting to describe. You know not when the killer will strike.

By the time we reached the bottom of the draw, it had become obvious that there was nothing left of Companies F and G to either rescue or support. The survivors were leaving the woods and coming back across the open ground under a hail of fire from the enemy counterattack. All we could do was to set up a line some two hundred yards from the edge of the woods to halt the German advance. It was a pitifully small group of GIs that passed through our line. They were mostly walking wounded, mud-covered, stunned, hollow-eyed, and exhausted from the hours in a hell of flying steel, impotent against the repeated close-in attacks of the German armor. Many of them no longer had their weapons or equipment. What at dawn had been two full reinforced companies were now reduced to some thirty-five effectives in Company F and a few more in G.

Our company line was stretched pretty thin at dusk, as we had dug into widely separated individual foxholes. Some German infantry emerged from the forest and fired their rifles in our direction. When we returned fire they melted into thickets, but we continued firing to discourage any reemergence. This was war, and it had to be done, but after emptying several clips, I really didn't want to know if I had hurt or killed anyone.

The higher-ups evidently wanted to know how close the Germans had positioned themselves and decided to send a three-man patrol to find out. Who could be better than three men from the special night mission squad that had been picked from the special night mission platoon that had been picked from the entire regiment?

Guess who won the three lucky numbers out of our squad: me and two other eighteen-year-old replacements by the names of Rose and

O'Connell. It was with Pat O'Connell that I was later to form an enduring friendship. When I think now of the tremendous odds against my number being chosen out of four thousand in the regiment I should be able to wipe them out in Las Vegas.

We blacked our faces, and when it was completely dark, we crossed the open ground and entered Bannholz Woods. We proceeded as stealthily and silently as possible, three abreast separated only by several feet, as that was as far as we could see. I've forgotten if anyone was in command. It wasn't Pat, and it certainly wasn't me, as I was never given command of anything at all during the time I was in the army. If anyone was in command, it must have been Rose. After all, they had taken away his M1 rifle and given him a grease gun, a fully automatic affair with a fold-out stock sometimes carried by tankers.

After moving some distance, all three of us at the same time felt the ground rise sharply beneath our feet. It was some sort of an enemy emplacement! Before we could think, muffled German voices came from right ahead of us. We were frozen. If I had been so inclined, I could have crawled a few feet forward, fished around, and probably tickled one of them under the chin. I was not so inclined; I was petrified. If there had been a hero in our trio, he could have lobbed a hand grenade in the general direction of the voices. Of course, if he had missed, they could have shot us.

This would have been no place for even whispered discussion, such as, "Hey, Rose, you're in command. All they asked us to do is to find out where they are, and we've done it. They're here! I vote we withdraw immediately." With Rose retorting, "Not yet, Kingsbury, I'm standing here meditating on whether or not to obtain more pertinent information."

Thoughts of any philosophical discussion became academic, as Rose had never learned to stiffen his forefinger, place it under his nose, and press firmly backward. All of a sudden, he let go with a great big sneeze. Beyond a shadow of a doubt, somewhere up there in the celestial ethereal regions floating around is an unwritten, immutable law that says, "When you are ten feet from the enemy in complete darkness and somebody sneezes, without a moment of hesitation everybody turns tail and runs like hell."

Did you ever try running full steam through a pine forest on a totally dark night? I'd like to say we cleared a path in front of us, which might have been true for the small bushes, but the trees were something else.

If we didn't bang into them headlong, we ricocheted hard to the left or right. After finally making it back to our lines, we reported to the officers though suffering from severe cases of tree battering. We told them an estimated location and distance of the Germans, which seemed to satisfy them, although to me the whole thing appeared a bit unnecessary. From what I had seen earlier in the day, there was no question in my mind about them being out there; there was no need to go out and rub noses with them to prove it.

Though I was later called upon to join lateral night patrols to contact adjoining units or forward patrols during the day, this was the only time I had to do a black-faced act at night, for which I am truly grateful.

Unfortunately, there were many hours still to go in my first night on line. Released from my mission, I was free to return to the warmth, safety, and comfort of the foxhole I had dug a few hours earlier. Ha! Jumping into my foxhole that night was like jumping into my own private bathtub partly filled with ice water. By this time of year the snow had melted, but it rained frequently, and the ground water was only a few inches below the surface. Seepage necessitated constant bailing with your steel helmet.

An infantryman's first night in a foxhole on the front line is something special, and I often wonder how many stories could be told by the thousands of men who experienced such a night. Fears loom way out of all proportion to reality. Shells constantly passing over my head produced the weirdest effect imaginable. These were the big boys from both sides, which were not wasted on the infantrymen but were destined to land on some installation or road intersection. They made swishing sounds, and it seemed as if I were on the floor of a vast ocean of air with ships passing over in both directions.

Loneliness of a deep order gripped me, as with the overcast sky there was a total darkness, and my foxhole neighbors were at a considerable distance and beyond sight. The only light was the eerie, sporadic lightning flashes produced by the cannon firing in the far distance both front and rear. Directly to my front were some trees that I could faintly see during the flashes, appearing as something coming out of a hideous nightmare. Fear began to pile upon fear, and I could feel the presence of the German Ghost Division about to launch its night counterattack right over my foxhole. I thought I could catch glimpses of something, maybe figures lurking around the bases of the trees.

Then it happened! The trees began to move. I had always been and still am somewhat scientifically oriented and skeptical about things out of the ordinary, but I can certainly attest to the fact that under certain circumstances your eyes and mind can play tricks. The motion of the trees was slow and steady to the left, the motion reminding me somewhat of how after a long day's travel on the highway, you can still see the road moving in your mind, even though you are lying on a motel bed with your eyes closed. I had seen movies of Japs moving bushes as camouflage, but the size of these trees made that sort of thing impossible. To verify whether I was seeing what I thought I was seeing, I wrapped the strap of my rifle tightly around my arm and elbow and locked the butt to my shoulder. Taking careful aim on one of the trees during a sustained flash, I waited, knowing there was no way the rifle could move, but the tree did! I then knew my conscious mind could no longer control what my eyes would see.

The final event of the night brought me to the borderline between sanity and nervous breakdown. A ghostly call suddenly echoed through the night air in front of me. "Ameri-can-ers, Ameri-can-ers, ve vant to surrender. Ve are carrying a vounded Americaner officer." Over and over again the ghostly voice would call out, drawing out the words slowly, with the tail end of the words dropping down in pitch. I was in solitary confinement and had no one with whom to confer. The hair had risen on the back of my neck, and I felt this was some sort of ploy or foul trick on the part of the Ghost Division. To make matters more scary, if that were possible, after ceasing for a while, the voice started up again, only now it was in back of me! The voice finally stopped for good, and I spent the rest of the night under extreme stress and anxiety.

As dawn began to break my spirits began to revive. Even under an overcast sky, there is no way to express the feeling of going from night to day in a foxhole. Time and again I was later to experience the same feeling. With dawn came the knowledge that I was still alive, and with life there was hope.

As soon as possible I found out about the ghostly voice. It actually had been a small group of German soldiers who wanted to surrender. They had carried with them a wounded American officer as a means of safe passage. The foxholes were so far apart that the Germans had simply walked between them to our rear. There some of the more seasoned hands took them into custody.

This second day brought with it a minor counterattack by the German Wehrmacht, possibly a large combat patrol that had come down through the draw to the north of us. Here I was initiated regarding the Schmeisser, a German machine pistol that used a clip of thirty-two 9mm bullets, had a high rate of fire, and went "Buurrp," which gave it its nickname of "Burp" gun. One bullet came closer than I like to remember.

I had sought the privacy of a thicket of bushes and small trees for my morning call, when several bullets zipped in, one only a foot away. I've often thought there could be no more inglorious death scene than one in which you are squatting with your pants down. It was because of this kind of German patrol activity or maybe to straighten our line with adjoining units that we pulled back up the slope several hundred yards toward the Sinz-Bubingen Road.

The second night was an improvement, with only one major event. But for Rose and me it was quite an event. Before lights out the sergeants had been emphatically clear that we were still subject to possible German counterattack or particularly to some enemy patrol activity. Under no circumstances were we to leave our foxholes until dawn. In this way, any kind of movement seen would automatically be known to be German.

Though the artillery flashes were not as frequent as the night before, the night itself was utterly dark. Shortly after midnight, during one of the flashes, to my horror I thought I saw a man crouched at the base of a tree some thirty feet to my right front. I concentrated my vision in that direction, waited for the next flash, and there it was, the faint outline of a soldier wearing a helmet. I immediately aimed my rifle, took up the trigger squeeze, and waited for the next flash to make any minor adjustment. Before the flashes returned, however, it dawned upon me that I was having hallucinations as I'd had the night before, and I lowered my rifle. A long string of flashes followed, and the man was still there. After several seconds he got up and walked across in front of me to my left! It was a GI! It was Rose, who, thinking he had heard a sound, had come forward to have a better look down the slope.

Rose had made a colossal blunder, and it almost had cost him his life. If it had been my third or fourth night on line I would have squeezed off a shot that would have blasted him into eternity. Only the hallucinations of the first night had saved him on the second. Maybe God was working in strange ways.

The experience was one of those things that has become a recurring memory to me down through the years. Life and death hinge upon the slightest twist of fate. Our very existence hangs from a spider's thin silken thread.

The next five days were spent dodging a lot of artillery shells and digging new foxholes every so often as we made minor moves of a few hundred yards either laterally along the slope or up or down the slope. I presume the purpose of moving was to hook in better with the units on our left or right. I say "presume" because the higher-ups for some inexplicable reason never saw fit to confer with me on their strategies. In recalling events, one of the biggest problems is to correlate my memories exactly with certain locations or towns. Since childhood I have loved to pore over maps, but did they ever once give me a map and orient me to my location? No.

I really didn't need to know where I was or where I was going, as they always graciously took care of this for me. There are many people, including myself, who believe that God has a plan for each day of our lives, but he gives us the freedom of other options if we desire. The army was exactly like this; just leave out the part about the options.

The fear of German counterattack was always upon us, so we got little rest or sleep. One night, during a hard rain, four or five of us crawled under the bed of a knocked-out truck. For me this was a bit ironical, as I had spent a good deal of my early years playing soldier in an old rusty steel truck bed in back of my father's shop. It probably had been put there by the garage people next door south. In my wallet, among pictures of Mary Jo and of my family, was a photo taken of me at age five or six, in front of the shop's double doors with my dog, Chief, at my side. On my hip was a toy pistol and holster, on my shoulder a toy rifle, and on my head a real World War I steel British helmet that someone had given me. By the hour, from within the truck bed and with this equipment, I would fend off the kaiser's advancing legions, using the sides as parapets.

I wasn't in this particular truck bed, I was under it. Lying down, at that. I think the reason my memory of this occasion is so vivid is that it was the only time during the war I ever received a pat on the back. Not that I ever deserved one, mind you, because at best I never did more than my duty. The praise arose through the fact that I fell sound asleep with lightning and artillery flashing while the others were nervously watching for any patrol activity. I had roused up enough to hear one of them say, "Look at that Kingsbury. He must have nerves of steel to sleep like a baby with all this going on."

The truth of the matter was that I felt there were enough eyes watching and was using sleep as a form of escape. I later honed this ability to perfection. At a moment's notice, safety permitting, I could drop off to sleep and in my dreams escape from war's realities. Of course I didn't explain this to the fellows under the truck bed. You have to get a few strokes whenever you can.

Though I didn't know the reason for it at the time, during this period the Twentieth Corps, which included our division, was engaged in a massive long-range softening-up process for its intended all-out offensive. Not only at Bannholz Woods, but in adjacent areas as well, the German defenders were receiving such concentrations of artillery and mortar fire as they had never known. German prisoners later captured by the regiment kept asking to see the American "automatic artillery." I estimated at the time that the Germans caught ten shells for every one they sent over to us. As the ones they were sending us were jarring me into a nervous wreck, I remember actually feeling sorry for the poor Joe on the other side who was the recipient of all that hell and wondering how he managed to retain his sanity.

To make matters worse for the Germans, the air force sent squadrons of P-47s and P-51s to strafe and bomb. As the planes maneuvered in huge vertical circles in ferris-wheel fashion in front of me, it was as if I were on the front row of a gigantic circus. I never had the experience, but I know to be strafed would be terrifying. A foxhole would be of little protection with bullets coming straight down.

The planes also showered the enemy with surrender leaflets and safe-conduct passes. These proved more and more effective as the days went by, and increasing numbers of deserters walked into the American lines. They were tired of defending the Saar-Moselle triangle, which many of them considered a hopeless task. They were also tired of fighting the Ninety-fourth Division, whom Axis Sally had dubbed "Roosevelt's Butchers." Maybe this name had psyched out some of the Germans in the same way that "Ghost Division" had affected me.

The division had been christened by Axis Sally in the middle of January, when the third battalion of my regiment took Nennig for the first time. As frequent German combat patrols were driven out and infiltrating groups of the enemy were hunted down, the number of corpses increased. Since there was no possible way of evacuating these bodies, they were collected and laid out neatly in one of the houses. After the enemy retook the town, Axis Sally in Berlin reported that these German dead were prisoners of war murdered in cold blood.

It was also during this period of being continually half frozen and wet, under great stress and getting little rest, that I contracted a severe chest cold. The platoon medic sent me to the company aid station, but they weren't about to let anybody off the line unless he was carried off. I wasn't even familiar with the term then, but I must have had walking pneumonia. More then anything else, the enervating congestion was to plague me the next few weeks.

As if this weren't enough, my physical condition was further complicated by frozen feet. The condition had developed gradually during the first week on line, with my feet constantly being in the wet mud at the bottom of a foxhole. We carried extra socks in our packs, and theoretically we were supposed to change them twice a day. I know of no one who changed them even once. Who'd want to be caught with his bare feet hanging out in the event of a counterattack?

On February 17 we were relieved for two days' rest and marched to some small town, probably Sinz. During this march, the pain became excruciating. It felt like my feet had been chopped off, and I was walking on two raw stumps. Trench foot and frozen feet claimed many casualties in the division during January and the first part of February, and by rights I should have been one of them. After being checked by the company medics I was sent to battalion aid, where the doctor there pronounced my feet frozen and ordered me to be evacuated. From there I had to pass through regimental aid on the way to the hospital. For what reason the regimental commander, Col. Harold H. McClune, was in the regimental aid station I'll never know. Probably to chew the fat with the medical officers.

As I came into the room and sat down in a chair to be examined, he was sitting just a few feet to my left. At that close range, at least in the eyes of an eighteen-year-old, the distance between me, a buck private, and him, a full colonel with eagles, was comparable to that of an ant looking up to the top of a tall oak tree. Besides, he was heavily built, looking like he might make a good wrestler. To me, his face was faintly reminiscent of a bull, which in his position might have been a good thing, as he had to be tough.

As the doctor looked at my feet, Colonel McClune started quizzing me. I'll have to admit that he spoke to me in a soft voice. Under some circumstances he might have been a kind bull. He asked, "Have you been changing your socks twice a day like you're supposed to?" I replied, "No, sir," and went on to explain that we had been constantly moving around and were in fear of a counterattack at any moment. When I had finished, he looked at the medical officer and said, "Send him back!" I wondered what he would have said if I had lied and said, "Yes, sir," to the two-socks-a-day inquiry. Probably, "Good boy—send him back!"

Looking at the situation from my present vantage point, I concede that had I been in his position, I probably would have acted in a similar manner. His leadership capabilities were beyond question. He had an excellent regular army career record, which included earlier service in the Mexican campaign and in World War I. About a week after we met, he was wounded by mortars in both legs and the chest while personally directing the crossing of the Saar, and he was unable to return to the regiment for three months. He was responsible for the lives of thousands of men, and this responsibility must have weighed heavily on him. The casualties were very heavy at this time, and all commanders were desperately trying to maintain a semblance of strength in their organizations. He was looking at the overall picture while I was focused on my own very narrow and selfish point of view.

In a way he was right, because after a few days of hobbling around, I became somewhat of an effective again, my main trouble being my chest cold.

Despite my so-called mature outlook, there are times in the wee small hours when I'm reliving some of these experiences, and I return to the regimental aid room and see the eighteen-year-old boy in the presence of his colonel. I hear the words, "Send him back!" The feelings of the youth resurface, and once again I think about full Colonel McClune—the sonuvabitch!

I returned, dejected, to my unit, but my spirits revived to some degree as we got to spend the next two nights inside the kind of walk-in basement of a large chateau in the town of Sinz. We slept on the floor, and the place was only dimly lit by some kerosene lamps. Under other circumstances it would have been a miserable, spooky place to spend the night, but considering my accommodations of the previous seven days, I felt that I had been put up in the Waldorf Astoria.

Our company was now in reserve while F and G covered the front line, so at least there was now time and opportunity to write Mary Jo a letter. On February 18 I struggled hard to be cheerful as I told her, "It's been somewhat tough lately, not getting any sleep some nights and having to stay in muddy foxholes. However, when a shell comes in your direction you forget about the mud and just dive in. Now that I've been on line for awhile I've gotten the Combat Infantryman's Badge which pays ten more bucks a month. I will also have a Pfc. Rating starting next month. In all I will get $74.80 a month. How about that? I'll be a millionaire before I know it. There's not much more I can tell you except that I miss you very much, Jo. Maybe it won't be too long before this war's over. I hope so, anyway. Lots of love, Dickie."

Mary Jo had easily picked up on the pessimistic tone of the letters I had written in January and during the first part of February. My letter of the 18th evidently relieved her mind to some extent as she received it and answered on March 1, "By the time you get this you'll already be a Pfc. I'm proud of you, fella. Shall I start addressing your letters to General Kingsbury, to keep up with your promotions? I'm only kidding about that General stuff—when you get to be a millionaire on that $74.80 a month, I'll still crave ya, boy, even if you're only a Lt. Colonel!"

She continued, "I feel relieved now—your letter sounded like *you*. There's something very cruel and hard to understand about life nowadays—a life that has placed sweet guys like you in a position where you talk as casually about a shell and a foxhole as you once did about dances, and homework. I'm glad that you are able to write about it casually—it shows you're not letting it get you down. I don't think I expected you to get a morbid viewpoint or anything, but I guess all those who just sit and wait, worry about how the fighting ones will be affected. Now I'm completely reassured—just that one crack about your pay really eased my mind. Even your little remark (about being a millionaire and having no time) really got a bigger laugh than it deserved, I was so glad to see it."

Perhaps in an attempt to cheer me up, she regaled me with a couple of stories about life on the home front. Silk stockings were but a fond memory, and the new nylons (which had been too expensive for her) were gone, as the armed forces needed the nylon for parachutes and other things, so she was reduced to wearing rayon hosiery. The big problem was that the rayon thread had very little resilience, and when you sat for a while and then stood up, the knees were so baggy "you could smuggle a grapefruit in them." Rationing of leather shoes also presented problems, and she had to supplement her footwear with nonrationed fabric shoes with synthetic soles. Some of these shoes weren't too bad, but she had been wearing a pair one day when a rainstorm hit just as she was walking home from the bus. By the time she got home the soles had come unglued and were flopping in the water!

After writing my letter to Mary Jo I received the good news that the next morning, February 19, the entire division was to go on the attack. The so-called offensive defense was ended. Thrusts by reinforced battalions with limited objectives were a thing of the past. This time the goal was to crack the Siegfried Switch Line once and for all. I say it was good news. It was good news for some. I'll never forget Gus Graham smiling and saying, "I'd rather be on the attack than sitting around taking it any time." I tended to disagree with him. Though it was no fun to cringe in a foxhole and try to crawl up inside your steel helmet when the shelling was going on, at least it seemed the natural thing to do. To have to get out of your foxhole when your whole being cried out for protection always seemed to me to be an inherent violation of nature. For Gus, to be on the attack meant that the war would be over just that much sooner. Wars are won by men such as he.

That night Lieutenant Ike spoke to a group of us GIs. The words he spoke caused me to bring to bear all of my moral, ethical, and religious values, and they will be imprinted on my memory forever. From within the context of our anticipated advance during the next few days, and from within his bitter experience of the previous weeks, he said, "As far as I'm concerned, personally, you do not have to take any prisoners, because the way I look at it, if it wasn't for them we wouldn't be here."

There was no talk among us afterward concerning this statement. I guess each of us had to run it through his own value system. For me the ramifications were rampant. Could there be a time when we would be moving so fast that it would be impossible to take prisoners to the rear or leave them for fear of having the enemy behind us? Would there be a time when they wanted to lay down their arms that we would continue firing, forcing them to defend themselves? Though the implication was not to shoot prisoners after they had been taken, we were still given a license to commit a form of murder.

It should be added that Lieutenant Ike himself, though he had opportunities, never committed any impropriety. Only the words were said, which goes to show that *not* to practice what you preach isn't always bad. The words were his own personal "goof," as I, too, certainly had many personal "goofs" brought about largely if not almost entirely by the unusual circumstances of the war.

I have referred to this matter primarily, I think, to show that there need not be any correlation between license and action and also to show the intrinsic values that lay in the hearts of at least a small cross section of the American citizenry called upon to serve their country during World War II.

At four o'clock on the morning of February 19 began the all-out division attack on the Siegfried Switch Line. During the previous hours of darkness, the three regiments had been massed abreast along a three-mile section in the center of the twelve-mile division front. The other nine miles were thinly covered by the Fifth Ranger Battalion on the east and a few divisional special units on the west. The First Battalion of the 376th was assigned the task of taking Bannholz Woods, while the Third Battalion was given the Woods of Adenholz and Geisbusch. My battalion, the Second, was temporarily in reserve.

In the interest of surprise, no artillery had been fired before the time of the attack. At four o'clock they began the now-famous fifteen-thousand-round barrage for a single division attack. There had been a vast fire-support plan worked out by Brig. Gen. Julius E. Slack, the commanding general of Twentieth Corps artillery, and Brig. Gen. Louis J. Fortier, the Ninety-fourth Division artillery commander, and their staffs.

The regimental cannon companies had been attached to the division artillery along with infantry antitank guns and the 774th Tank Destroyer Battalion, all of which were firing as field artillery. These units engaged all targets up to five thousand yards in advance of the division front. Beyond this point all of the available artillery of the Twentieth Corps engaged all known enemy command posts for fifteen minutes, in order to disrupt their communications and command. Following this, corps fire fell on hostile battery positions for one and a half hours. Then for the next ten hours fire was directed against the main routes of approach to the battle area. This fire on road intersections prevented the Germans from reinforcing and resupplying their front-line positions and also forced them to abandon the majority of their wheeled vehicles and heavy weapons when they began to retreat.

As the assault battalions of three regiments began their attack, the German artillery opened up as usual, but this time there was no way they could concentrate every cannon, mortar, and tank against just one battalion, as they had in the past.

The First Battalion advanced into Bannholz Woods on a narrow front to avoid the Schu mines on either side. The overcast sky, from which a light drizzle was falling, made it so dark between artillery flashes that it was impossible for them to see more than a yard or two ahead. Fortunately, the enemy could see no better in the inky darkness, and showing the effects of the previous week's bombardment as well as the present's, they chose not to reveal their positions by firing on the unseen attackers as they advanced.

The battalion infiltrated the northern edge of the woods and dug in. The Germans, now realizing that the Americans were to their rear and the supporting American tanks were beginning to crash into the woods to their front, knew that they were doomed and began to surrender in groups. By eight o'clock the long-contested Bannholz Woods was at last in American hands. Further to the west, though suffering heavy casualties from minefields, the Third Battalion also took Adenholz and Geisbusch Woods.

Around noon the First Battalion advanced toward the northern portion of Munsingen Ridge, and my Company E was ordered into the northern edge of Bannholz Woods to temporarily fill the gap between the First and Third Battalions. We dug our foxholes in the open ground directly in front of the woods, with several knocked-out German tanks to our rear. As daylight turned into dusk, we still caught some German artillery and mortar fire. Later, after it had gotten dark, Neal, one of my fellow replacements in the platoon, was wounded by a "screaming meemie," and a volley from our own artillery landed within twenty-five yards.

Fortunately, most of us were in our foxholes at the time of this miscalculated salvo, and little damage was done. One nice thing about an artillery shell, if that's possible, is that it explodes upon contact, and the shrapnel has a slight upward trajectory. Unless the shell hits close, you are relatively safe in a foxhole or even lying on the ground. As the shell whistles in you have one brief split second's warning to duck or hit the deck. As you walked along you soon learned to keep one eye trained on the terrain, looking for the slightest dip or ditch and if possible to walk beside it. To this day, though no longer looking for depressions, I still have to fight to keep myself from staring down at the ground as I move along.

There is another kind of artillery fire called "time fire," in which the shell bursts some twenty or thirty feet before reaching the ground, and you have nowhere to turn. I consider myself lucky not to have been exposed to this type until my last day on line.

During the early evening some of us got out of our holes to stretch our legs in the dark. It was here that some of the older men taught me how, by cupping my hands, to smoke without showing any light that might attract enemy fire. Though I had been a light smoker before entering the army, I now smoked with a passion. I particularly experienced great joy in smoking at night in a foxhole—looking at the little black specks that hovered over the red glow beneath. It was just a little thing, but it was warm and comforting in a world which at that moment was offering nothing that I wanted.

By the evening of February 19, the other two regiments to the east, the 301st and the 302nd, had met with success equal to that of the 376th, and the center of the Siegfried Switch Line was beginning to crumble.

Around midnight of that same evening my company was pulled back to the Sinz-Bubingen Road, put on trucks, and moved to the western flank of the division front, where we rejoined the other two line companies of our battalion, companies F and G. The mission of our battalion was to crack the line in the area of Kreuzweiler and Thorn. Our battalion was heavily reinforced by special units, including tanks. If successful in creating a breach, the Tenth Armored Division, to which the 376th Regiment was now attached, would pour through and quickly cut deep into the northern part of the Saar-Moselle triangle, preventing reinforcement to the center and eastern portions of the German line. This western section was flatter and much more geographically suitable to fast-moving armor than were the hilly sections to the east.

In the morning the usual heavy artillery preparation preceded our battalion attack on Kreuzweiler. F and G were the assault companies, while my Company E was to follow. F and G had recently taken on 60 new replacements each, for a total of 120, mostly eighteen-year-olds. They momentarily froze, and we wondered about the cause of the delay. This was not an act of cowardice by any means. To understand it, you would have to see the smoke, hear the noise, and feel the concussion from the tumultuous artillery barrage. The mind is willing, but the body doesn't respond.

At a Ninety-fourth Division reunion in the early 1980s, I had an opportunity to sit down and visit with Arthur Dodson. At that time he was a retired army colonel. He had been a first lieutenant and executive officer of my Company E. Then he had taken over command of the company when Captain Darrah was wounded and led us into Bannholz Woods for my first day of combat. Very soon afterward he was promoted to captain and given command of Company G.

I asked him about the Kreuzweiler incident. He told me that he literally had to pistol-whip the steel helmets of some of the new replacements to get the men to come out of their foxholes. But once they were up and rolling they did just fine.

Though stiff resistance was met in both the woods and town of Kreuzweiler, before the end of the day they fell into American hands. My platoon was on the west flank of the battalion, and that afternoon I was part of a probe patrol sent into Thorner Woods to see how strongly the Germans were lodged there. The Ninety-fourth Division book says that our patrol captured a machine gun nest and its crew, which in a sense is correct. However, it would be more accurate to say they handed it to us and scared the pants off us in the process. As we approached the position it was so well camouflaged that we didn't see it. If they had opened up on us while we were in the open, I doubt if any of us would have escaped. Fortunately, they had had all the war they wanted, and as soon as we were on top of them they arose in front of us with their hands up, yelling "Kamerad!" There were about six of them dressed in camouflage suits, and I was assigned to take them back to the rear.

As I marshaled them along I don't know who was more scared, them or me. After awhile, however, I remember feeling a sense of power as I directed them this way and that with my rifle. I held the authority of life and death over them, and we all knew it. Maybe holdup men enjoy this feeling as much as the money they take.

With the fall of Kreuzweiler, there was nothing left of the Switch Line. After weeks of cruel struggle, the stubborn line had bent and then cracked. By the evening of February 20, the tanks of the Tenth Armored were already far into the Saar-Moselle triangle, and the Germans were in full retreat all the way along the division front. It now became a race to see how many of them could make it safely to the east side of the Saar River before being captured or destroyed.

That night our squad slept in the hayloft of a barn. I was dead tired, and the hay was an unbelievable luxury. As we bedded down we were told that we would have six hours to sleep before having to move out again. I remember thinking how nice it was to have such a nice long stretch like that, compared to the one hour or two hours of other nights. Everything is relative, I guess, and ever since then, whenever I see that I'm only going to have six hours to sleep, I recall the hayloft, and it keeps me from feeling sorry for myself.

On the morning of the twenty-first, our battalion advanced, all three companies abreast in line in extended order. In this way we could cut the largest swath possible. Early in the day, in Kretenbusch Woods, my company found the remnants of a German artillery battalion. Effects of American counterbattery fire were clearly evident. The woods were littered with dead, and the enemy guns were twisted masses of wreckage.

In an abandoned machine gun nest I saw a large number of grenades, called potato mashers, with wooden handles, and concussion grenades that looked like large, smooth black eggs. I was very thankful not to have been the recipient of one of these things.

For infantry we moved fast that day, covering more than twenty miles before reaching Mannebach much after dark. The battalion met with only light pockets of rearguard resistance as the vast bulk of German forces were scrambling for the east bank of the Saar. I had great difficulty keeping up, as my feet were still bothering me and carrying one hundred pounds of clothing and equipment didn't help. My chest cold completely enervated me, and I became winded when I had to move fast or up a grade. Getting winded when I ran had been a problem for me even in basic training, let alone under the present conditions. Despite introspective feelings of guilt in other areas, I can truthfully say to myself that I did my dead-level best to keep up. With the previous problem they knew I had had with my feet, I could probably have gotten away with faking a total inability to walk. I certainly knew how to goldbrick. In my letters to Mary Jo during basic training, I bragged on a number of occasions about my great prowess in this area.

Somehow it was all different now. More than anything else I wanted to get off line, but only if it was fair and square and rightfully deserved. I think more than anything else, what makes a rifle squad or platoon tick is the spirit of comradeship that develops. The flag-waving is far behind, and even the overall view, meaning, and purpose of the war are forgotten and submerged by thoughts of not wanting to let your buddy down.

At one time during this fast-moving day our squad stopped at a farmhouse for about thirty minutes. I went upstairs looking for a bedroom. At the head of the stairs was a small cubbyhole-like room with a single bed, probably used by a child or youth. Most important of all, however, was the fact that the bed was of the fluffed-up feather bed type. I had never been on one before or since, but I plopped down on it, muddy boots and all, and it was heaven. I began to fantasize that they would forget me when the outfit moved on, and how nice a place this would be to spend the rest of the war. It wasn't long, though, before the sergeant yelled from downstairs, "Let's move out!" and I bounded out of bed on the double.

The distance between a private and an officer was *quite* a distance. It was also discouraging, since in my childhood I had always been "King of the World" or at least a general. To be a private is quite an experience in itself—like lying flat on your back in the sediment in the bottom of a fishbowl, looking up at all the activity. Everybody that counts is above you. You would talk to the noncoms and even the second lieutenants to some extent as if you were their equal, and they were more than friendly. But when they spoke an order, regardless of how gently, you followed it immediately and without question, as if the Lord from his holy mountain had commanded it on tablets of stone. To disobey or even to think about disobeying would never enter your head, as it was now war and not basic training.

Me at six years old, wearing WWI British steel helmet and carrying a toy rifle and pistol, with our police dog, Chief

Me at seventeen

Mary Jo at fifteen

Central High School, Kansas City, Missouri, 1943

Dear Mary Jo,

Our friendship through this year has begun and deepened. I hope that next year it will ripen and develop even further. Your personality has drawn me to you closer & closer. I do hope you feel the same way. I want you to always remember me and even love me.

Lots of luck and love – Always

Bob

Samuely

Dear Mary Jo,

Our friendship has been rather brief, but I think you are awfully cute and sweet. Here's to you. Aim high. Lots of luck.

Gloria Spencer

Dear Mary Jo,

I haven't known you long (all of 15 minutes) but it doesn't take you long to see that you're a cute, sweet, charming girl. I'm really looking forward to being in some of your classes next year.

Best wishes to a swell girl,

Dick Kingsbury

Dear Mary Jo,

Boy, we've certainly had the times up here at choir and school. You've "bopped" me around and I've "bopped" you around. Oh Me! Such is life. But you are a swell gal and will go far with your looks, personality too. Best of luck, success and happiness.

Marvin B. Lakeman

Mary Jo's yearbook, signed by me, 1942

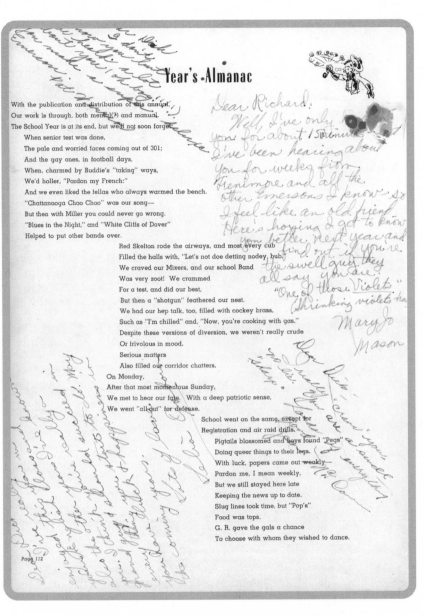

Year's Almanac

With the publication and distribution of this annual,
Our work is through, both mental(?) and manual.
The School Year is at its end, but we'll not soon forget.
When senior test was done,
The pale and worried faces coming out of 301;
And the gay ones, in football days,
When, charmed by Buddie's "taking" ways,
We'd holler, "Pardon my French:"
And we even liked the fellas who always warmed the bench.
"Chattanooga Choo Choo" was our song—
But then with Miller you could never go wrong.
"Blues in the Night," and "White Cliffs of Dover"
Helped to put other bands over.
Red Skelton rode the airways, and most every cub
Filled the halls with, "Let's not doe detting nodey, bub."
We craved our Mixers, and our school Band
Was very zoot! We crammed
For a test, and did our best,
But then a "shotgun" feathered our nest.
We had our hep talk, too, filled with cockey brass,
Such as "I'm chilled" and, "Now, you're cooking with gas."
Despite these versions of diversion, we weren't really crude
Or frivolous in mood.
Serious matters
Also filled our corridor chatters.
On Monday,
After that most momentous Sunday,
We met to hear our fate. With a deep patriotic sense,
We went "all-out" for defense.
School went on the same, except for
Registration and air raid drills.
Pigtails blossomed and boys found "Pegs"
Doing queer things to their legs.
With luck, papers came out weakly—
Pardon me, I mean weekly,
But we still stayed here late
Keeping the news up to date.
Slug lines took time, but "Pop's"
Food was tops.
G. R. gave the gals a chance
To choose with whom they wished to dance.

Page 112

My yearbook, signed by Mary Jo, 1942

71

Basic training,
Ft. McClellan,
Alabama, 1944

Gus Graham, my first
squad leader, at Lam-
paden, Germany

Rifle squad, Lampaden, Germany, about March 15, 1945.
I am in the top row, second from the left. Three of the
men were killed and four were wounded one week later.

Pat O'Connell, Wuppertal, Germany

Former Gestapo headquarters, Wuppertal, Germany.
We used it as a prison for 1,200 German war criminals.

Mural from the former Gestapo headquarters in Wuppertal, Germany

Mary Jo had just turned seventeen when this picture
was taken. I carried this in my wallet during the war.

Ben Siegel, my second squad leader. I am on the right with my back turned. Tipton is in the rear; he was killed one week later.

Phil Phares and me in Volyne, Czechoslovakia, August 1945

Bob Hope arriving in Winterburg, Czechoslovakia, August 1945, for a USO show

Jerry Colonna on the airstrip in Winterburg, Czechoslovakia, sitting in a small aircraft behind an unidentified
pilot. The side window panel has been folded up.

Me down to 118 pounds after an operation, taken in a photo booth near the hospital at Verdun, France

In front of the statue of Louis XIV at Versailles, September 1945. Ralph Brunn is in the bottom row, first on the right; I am in the top row, fifth from the right.

Me at the Trocadero Gardens, Paris, France, September 1945

Mary Jo and me, engagement picture, November 1945

Chapter Six

After a couple of hours of rest in Mannebach, the battalion was ordered to proceed to Ayl on the Saar River. We arrived there shortly after midnight and joined up with the First and Second Battalions. You'd think after taking the entire Saar-Moselle triangle the Ninety-fourth Division would be allowed a few days' rest before crossing the Saar to attack the main Siegfried Line on the east bank. But General Patton didn't see it that way. In fact, "Anxious George" didn't want to wait a few hours, and ordered the division to cross the Saar at four o'clock that same morning. Our regiment, the 376th, was to cross at Ayl, while the 301st and 302nd were to do the same at towns further to the south.

I guess General Patton wanted to catch the Germans off guard, figuring that they would assume that we wouldn't attack for some time, with the main Siegfried defense just beyond the river. The only thing that kept the attack from coming off at four o'clock, at least in our regimental sector, was that even George Patton, let alone his men, couldn't walk on the water. The retreating Germans had blown all the bridges, and the river was wide, deep, and swollen this time of year. Assault boats had been promised for crossing, but none had arrived, so the regiment was dispersed in buildings throughout Ayl for most of the daylight hours of the 22nd.

Our platoon stayed for a few hours in a large stone house. I remember we had to cross a street to get to it, running one at a time at irregular intervals to avoid sniper fire from the Germans across the river.

Inside the house we had some time to rest and talk. I remember Moon Welling talking about his family, which seems like a very little thing to remember, since just about everybody talked about their families. Of all the million little insignificant happenings that hang down from the ceiling of the tunnel of life, like grapes suspended by tiny stems, why is it we pick one out every now and then to hold onto? I think I know why. Moon had just received word that his wife had delivered a baby. Everyone was congratulating him on having a baby girl. In a joking manner he said, "It's easy to make a girl, because you have the pattern right in front of you." Moon was killed a few days later by machine gun fire, and my mind reverted to what he had said earlier. I thought of the family that would never see him again. This is why you didn't want to get to know the others too well. To lose a face is one thing. To lose what is behind the face is another.

Around noon on the 22nd, a small number of assault craft arrived, but they were insufficient for a crossing operation involving a full infantry regiment and its resupply until such time as a bridge could be constructed. However, they were enough for General Patton. He visited the Tenth Armored command post in town, which was next door to that of the 376th, and was extremely perturbed that the crossing had not been initiated. He gave his order to the Tenth Armored, which didn't take long to get next door to Colonel McClune, for the 376th Regiment to "Cross at once."

Smoke generators went into action, and soon the river valley was covered with dense, billowing white smoke, which denied the Germans all observation as the assault companies moved to the river. Unfortunately, the generators, many of which had been damaged by the enemy's constant machine gun fire, ceased to function one by one. A slight breeze dispelled the smoke, and before long the enemy had an unobstructed view of the crossings. All hell broke loose as every German machine gun, mortar, and artillery piece within range fired upon the two assault companies, C and L.

Amid a hail of machine gun bullets, Colonel McClune moved about on the coverless flats, personally encouraging and urging his men to renewed efforts in achieving the crossing. But it was all to no avail. Finally, to avoid a slaughter, the crossing was halted, and the troops were ordered back to Ayl. In addition to the heavy casualties in the two assault companies, many of whom were unable to leave or be carried from the river area until after dark, not a single boat escaped destruction.

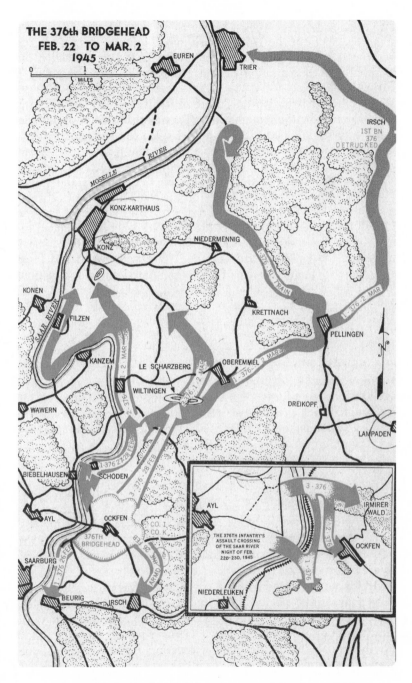

The 376th bridgehead, February 22 to March 2, 1945

After being informed of the temporary setback, the Tenth Armored Division tried to pin Colonel McClune down to the earliest possible time the regiment could resume the crossing attempt. The colonel let 'em have it good by replying, "One hour after I receive sufficient boats."

About ten o'clock that night, a sufficient shipment of assault boats arrived in town, and with the fog settling in the river valley, conditions seemed ideal for crossing. The Third Battalion was to seize the steep bluffs north of the town of Ockfen, while the First Battalion was to claim the high ground to the south. My battalion was to assault Ockfen itself, which was about a quarter mile on beyond the river. By four o'clock the next morning, the 376th Regiment had crossed the Saar.

Colonel McClune again directed the crossing personally, but this time his luck ran out; during a terrific mortar concentration, he was wounded in both legs and the chest. Lieutenant Colonel Anderson, the executive officer, then took command of the regiment.

As my company moved up to the river from Ayl we were hit with prearranged German artillery fire. They couldn't see us, but they knew just about where we would be crossing. After a period for reorganization, we loaded into the assault boats as fast as we could. The boats were plywood, flat-bottomed dories about twenty feet long, and each one held about ten infantrymen and two engineers. Each man was supplied with a paddle, very much like a canoe paddle, to move the boat forward while it was steered by one of the engineers from the stern. As we crossed, enemy machine guns firing at random in the darkness raised spray up and down the river.

After reaching the east bank we were supposed to assault Ockfen. There was just one catch. Before you could assault it, you had to find it, and that proved temporarily impossible. Because of the smoke and the fog, visibility was limited to a matter of feet. Control was difficult and progress slow. In several instances, groups returning with prisoners were being mistaken for the enemy and fired upon. It was a weird night. For some time my platoon was lost and would wind back and forth in a line running east and west, up a gulley and then down, each man sometimes holding on to the shoulder of the man in front of him in order to maintain visual contact.

At one point the front part of our line ran into a German machine gun, and the gunner opened fire. As the bullets went by I dove into a tiny creek to my right. Someone up front silenced the machine gun, and I crawled out, all wet and cold but in one piece. It's amazing what comfort you'll sacrifice under certain circumstances.

Another time our line was stopped, and we were just waiting. About ten or twelve feet to our right we could faintly make out the murky figures of soldiers going in the opposite direction. We assumed that it was the front part of our platoon line doubling back as it had done all night, with the lieutenant playing follow the leader. A moment later, however, some of the men behind us realized that the moving figures were a German patrol and took them prisoner. We found out later that the Germans had thought we were a hedgerow!

We returned to the river to move upstream and try to find Ockfen at another point. Once we got closer to the river we could clearly hear but not see in the foggy darkness. A member of one of the many special units attached to our regiment had evidently cracked under the psychological strain. Among the German prisoners being collected down at the river's edge he had found one wearing an American wrist watch. In loud, hysterical tones he was crying that the watch had been that of his dead buddy and that the German had killed him. In the darkness, his chance of recognizing the watch to be American, let alone his buddy's, was one in a million. Nevertheless, in his mind he was confronting his buddy's murderer, and we heard a carbine shot ring out. Strong verbal disapproval was expressed by all of the infantrymen within my earshot. Whatever was done or happened to the berserk GI, I have no way of knowing—perhaps nothing, in the unreal setting where the world was turned upside down.

By now the hours of eerie wandering in the foggy night and the extreme stress had taken their toll on my nerves. They had gone from bad to worse to shot. Invisible hands had slipped up along the sides of my head and under my helmet liner. Fingernails like razor blades had slit my scalp and peeled me all the way down like a banana, exposing the raw ends of pulsating nerves. Death was all around me, and I was part of it. Even in the daylight of the day before, my muddy hands had looked like the hands of the German corpses I had seen in the previous days. The murky fog, the complete darkness, and my shattered nerves had already placed me in "Sheol." The only thing left was oblivion.

In Ayl the day before, the squad had talked over how we were to assault any house in which there were determined defenders. My job was to use my rifle grenade launcher and fire a grenade through a window or to blow open a door, and then we would all rush in. I *knew* that in the process I would be shot and killed by the Germans. You must understand that on the level of feeling that I experienced this foggy night, I didn't *think* I was going to be killed, or *fear* that I was going to be killed, I *knew* I was going to be killed, which is a different kind of feeling altogether.

Farther south along the river, members of F Company had followed a railroad track through an underpass and located the valley that led east into Ockfen. Word came to us that Ockfen was located, and we would soon attack. Hurriedly, within the squad, nervous words reiterated the plan for attacking any stubborn house or building in the dark.

Someone said, "We'll all rush the house after Kingsbury fires a rifle grenade."

About then a voice came out of the dark, saying, "Yeah, if we can just get Kingsbury to keep up."

It was the voice of the only one who had taken cheap shots at me, particularly when I was struggling to keep up with the fast pace several days previously. He was only a little bit bigger than I, so I could hardly rate him as a first-class bully, but he had a propensity in that direction. I realize now that his snide remarks probably stemmed, at least in part, from his own nervousness. I had taken the earlier remarks in silence, but this was an entirely different setting. His sarcastic comment clawed down the raw ends of my exposed nerves, and I exploded into an act of which normally I would never be capable. I was soon going to die so nothing really mattered anyway. Holding my rifle upright and gripping it with both hands, I rammed the muzzle straight up under his chin, driving it deep into the soft triangular hollow of his jawbone, suspending him helplessly like a side of beef hanging from a meat hook, and from the very depths of my soul I cried out, "You goddam sonuvabitch, one more crack out of you and I'll blow your head off!"

Strangely enough, from that moment onward, through the rest of the war and all through the German and Czechoslovakian occupation that followed, we were never friends, but he and I got along just fine.

Company G had moved up on the hill north of Ockfen to secure our left flank. The balance of the battalion, Companies E and F and two heavy machine gun platoons from H, advanced over four hundred yards of flat marshland to the edge of town. Fortunately, daybreak had arrived by then, and despite the fact that the chemical warfare boys on the west side of the river were again laying in heavy smoke screens, we could at least see something.

Gus Graham was by now our squad leader, and as we advanced I was close on his heels. As we got to the first houses a German soldier with a rifle in his hands stepped around the corner of a house, and quick as a wink, Gus raised his rifle and shot him. As a youth when I would shoot bottles in a gulley with my .22 rifle, or targets out at the shooting gallery at Fairyland Park, the targets would always explode or immediately disintegrate. But this was different. The soldier let his rifle slip from his hands, and he just stood there, as if to say, "Can this be happening to me?" He slowly sank to his knees, then fell on his side and began moving his legs. I guess the Nazi supermen loomed before me, and fearing that he would rise up once more, I yelled at Gus, "Shoot him again, Gus, he's still moving!" All Gus did was to give a negative shake of his head.

In that one gesture, I think Gus in a sense preached more compassion than I was to do later in nine years from the pulpit. Many things were implicit. Never indulge in overkill. Don't kick anyone when he is down, even an enemy. Every human has the right to die with whatever dignity is available to him at that moment.

After a time our platoon and two platoons from Company F had taken possession of the west end of town by firing through doors, then rushing in to take prisoners. Our squad had gotten into a huge house we surmised had belonged to the burgomaster. The cellar contained a fine supply of wines of which I made mental note.

Suddenly we could hear the rumble of tanks from the east part of town. The noise grew louder as the tanks roared forward, throwing lead in all directions. Behind them were large numbers of German infantry. The bazooka teams that had been attached to our battalion went into action, but they were helpless against the bazooka skirts worn by the tanks and the cannon that were fired point-blank at the houses in which we were situated. We did the only sensible thing by pouring out the back door and running for the steep hill to the north of Ockfen, along with every other GI in the area, including those from platoons that hadn't yet gotten into town.

It's interesting that both the division and regimental books say the battalion "withdrew" to the hill. "Withdrew" is good military terminology that covers a multitude of sins. A layman would have said the battalion "ran for the hills." It's not often in modern warfare that you see an entire battalion spread out in the open in Civil War fashion, in mad flight from the enemy, but I saw it. Our motivation stemmed, of course, from the German tanks that were chasing us and spraying machine gun bullets every which way. We knew that if we could reach the safety of the hill the tanks would not dare follow, as our bazooka men would be able to peek under their bazooka skirts and blast away at their soft underbellies.

A more accurate description of our mad flight was later given in the regimental book by Capt. Robert Q. Smith, Jr., commander of Company H, the heavy weapons company. He had just placed a heavy machine gun section on the hill, overlooking the dense cloud of smoke put out by the chemical warfare boys, in order to fire on any movement in the west part of town. He was startled to see, emerging from the smoke, "the whole battalion swarming up the side of this steep—and I do mean steep—hill."

Later, in his report over the radio to higher headquarters, the battalion commander, Lieutenant Colonel Martin, was asked if his battalion was in any danger. He replied, "Nothing but mountain goats or scared infantrymen could ever climb this hill, and my whole damned battalion is up here."

It's also interesting that the division book says there were no fewer than sixteen German tanks involved while the regimental book says there were at least four. I've always wondered about it; this is quite a discrepancy. It only recently dawned on me that the probable reason is that no one, including myself, ever stopped long enough to look back and take a good count!

It's one thing to run for your life, but it's another to be unable to run. The distance from the town to the base of the hill was perhaps a quarter of a mile. After running about two-thirds of the distance I completely gave out from the effects of my chest cold. There comes a time when even adrenaline gives up the ghost. Where was that bundle of energy who had once brought Mary Jo home from a movie around midnight and then wanted to take her out again bowling, as places stayed open late because so many soldiers from area military installations came to town on weekend passes? Her mother said, "Is he out of his mind?" and the evening was ended.

The best I could do was walk, with others rushing past me. The terror that gripped me as I heard the machine guns firing to my back is beyond description. When I reached the steep hill and started climbing, I felt as if I were moving in slow motion, struggling vainly to reach even the first of the trenches the Germans had previously dug. As I clawed my way up to the trench, a GI rose up and exposed himself to fire, leaned way down, grasped my extended arm, and pulled me in. I then lay in the bottom of the trench, fighting for my breath like a fish lying on a riverbank.

Though all units were totally mixed up because of the frantic flight, the man who pulled me to safety was from my platoon but not in my squad. He was older, and I had only a nodding acquaintance with him. I never thanked him for what he did—I felt he might think it really wasn't so much, just one of those things you do when you're a member of the team—but my memory of him is imprinted as deeply as if Jesus Christ himself had leaned down from the parapets of heaven to reach for the extended arm of a lost sinner.

Before long the German tanks moved back into Ockfen, and under the cover of the dense smoke the battalion reorganized. The mix-up of men and units was unbelievable. For some time there was a mass swapping back and forth between trenches, like checkers players taking turns jumping over their opponents. Finally, everybody got back to his own company, platoon, and squad.

For several hours a moderate amount of American artillery fire was turned on the town, being ably directed and adjusted by our battalion officers, who now had clear visibility from their roost on top of the world. By early afternoon, however, Lieutenant Colonel Martin prepared us to face the inevitable. We would have to do what we were being paid for and once again attempt to take Ockfen.

Prior to the attack we had to move into position. All units had moved to the safety of the upper trenches but now had to be brought down to the lower ones. Since my platoon was one of the assault platoons, we headed for the first trench. Unfortunately, between trenches I tripped on a piece of low-strung barbed wire and fell flat on my face. My steel helmet came off and began rolling and bouncing down the hill. It bounced over the bottom trench and on down. When we reached the trench, one of the higher sergeants bawled out, "Kingsbury, go down there and get your @#$%&* helmet!"

This was one of life's lowest moments. Besides the humiliation of retrieving it in front of all the others, as far as I was concerned it was downright dangerous. The only logical thing to do was to pick it up as we went past, but I guess the sergeant thought it would destroy the décor of the initial advance if I didn't have on my helmet. So down I went to the bottom of the hill, retrieved my helmet, and scrambled back, fearing all the time that I'd get shot. It would have served the sergeant right if I had gotten shot—he would have had me on his conscience for the rest of his life. The big problem was that I was only eighteen. If I had known then what I know now, I would have told him to go down and get it himself and shove it you know where, figuring that at best it was a senseless order and, if necessary, I could easily defend myself in a court-martial.

Of course, I'll have to admit that if I had picked up the helmet on the way past and taken as long to adjust it to my head as I had done in basic training, the rest of the battalion would have been halfway through Ockfen by the time I had finished. I used to stand in front of the mirror in the latrine and work with it until I finally got it cocked at just the right angle to give me a rakish look.

The time of the attack was set for two fifteen. However, this time there would be tremendous artillery preparation to neutralize the German armor in Ockfen. Colonel Martin had come down to our trench to direct the artillery fire and by chance was only about fifteen feet to my right. This was the closest I had ever been to him, as a private's path didn't often cross that of a lieutenant colonel. It was quite an experience to hear him call for a "serenade," or TOT (time on target), on his radio, and to behold the holocaust that followed.

Every available piece of artillery for miles around was to be concentrated on the small town. Eight battalions of artillery participated in all. Firing first were the huge 240mms from miles back across the Saar. Then, at just the right time, these large shells were joined in flight by the 155s. Still later the close-in 105s fired in perfect timing to send their payload to add to the group. Even the Regimental Cannon Company, at much closer range, finally got into the act, some of which was with smaller bore.

At last the vast armada of death sailed in and exploded on the town like an atomic bomb. The enemy later said: "A tremendous artillery barrage landed on the town literally lifting it off its foundation and piling it in its own streets." The barrage was supposed to continue at maximum fire for ten minutes, but in half that time the effect of the concussion had become intolerable for us, despite the fact that we were a quarter of a mile away. Colonel Martin radioed for them to slow it down.

Then, as the sound of artillery subsided, there came a command that I heard only that one time during the war, but once in a lifetime is one time too many. The voices of unit commanders reverberated throughout the battalion: "Fix bayonets!" In basic training they told us that the sight of bayonets would strike terror in the hearts of the enemy. I can only give you my own solitary witness that for me, at least, the psychology had backfired. The ominous metallic clicking of hundreds of bayonets slamming into place struck terror in me! Then with my helmet on my head, so as not to destroy the décor of it all, the battalion poured out of the trenches in World War I fashion with fixed bayonets pointed straight ahead.

I couldn't think of anything worse than having to use a bayonet, except, of course, having one used on me. They were great for opening cans, but that was the end of it. I had already programmed into my thinking that in any close situation I would count shots, being careful not to fire more than six out of a clip before changing, in order to always have two in reserve. The only likely occasion for using a bayonet would be if you and an enemy were out of ammunition at the same time. If only one of the two were out, any prowess at bayonet fighting would be purely academic. "I stepped into the front of the house, with my rifle held level at the hip. The German did the same from the rear. We stared at each other. My rifle went 'click.' His rifle went 'click.' We both *charged*." It would never happen.

We advanced under the cover of artillery fire and with classic performance the fire lifted just as we reached the first building. Many of the houses and buildings were a shamble of wreckage and were starting to burn. Some of the German tanks had been destroyed by the TOT, and as we advanced we could hear the surviving panzers pulling out to the east. Of the German infantry that remained alive, most had taken refuge in cellars and were in a shocked and dazed condition. A few managed to run to their machine guns and commence firing, inflicting moderate casualties until they were quickly eliminated by accurately thrown grenades.

I would never attempt to throw a hand grenade, as I knew I could not throw it far enough to feel reasonably safe from fragments coming back in my direction. I well remembered my many humiliating experiences in summer, when the boys in the area would gather at Linwood Park to play baseball. Two leaders would choose up sides by the calling out of names. My name was never called because I was always the last one standing.

However, pulling a pin and throwing the grenade down the steps of a cellar was well within my capacity. In some of the damaged houses we had to search through the rubble to find the entrances to their cellars before throwing in hand grenades. This usually brought out "surrenderees" in a hurry.

One occasion was funny. After the grenade treatment by Chernak and me, a German sergeant waving a white handkerchief emerged from the cellar. One by one a large number of soldiers followed. Finally, after a good deal of hesitation and hearing no shots (which meant we weren't shooting prisoners that day), out came a big fat captain. Perhaps as a boy he had wanted to be in the navy and upheld the tradition that the captain should always be the last one to leave the ship. Lieutenant Ike ordered me to take the group to the rear. I marshaled them a very short distance down the street to the west, where someone took charge of them for the rest of the trip back to the river.

We took many prisoners that day, with resistance being spotty as we moved east through town, clearing house by house as we went. I noticed as we went by that the burgomaster's house with its wine cellar was still standing.

The houses that were still erect were of interesting construction. They each had a small attached barn, not much larger than an attached garage, with an inside door leading into the house. The livestock had gone with the residents, but the hayracks and the chickens had been left behind. We knew it might be days before any bridge could be built across the Saar, permitting the company kitchens to join us, so Gus Graham assigned me the job of gathering fresh eggs. In one of the houses I found a huge woman's purse; it was about half the size of a shopping bag, and I took it to carry the eggs. As soon as our squad would take a house by firing through the doors and windows, then moving in to root out prisoners, I'd rush into the barn and start rooting through the hay for eggs. After finding a few I'd rush out to rejoin the squad moving up the street. I'm glad the war newsreels never caught this act. I'm sure I made a queer sight advancing up the streets of Ockfen with fixed bayonet, a woman's purse filled with eggs hanging from my left arm.

To this day, whenever Mary Jo hands me her purse, filled with a ton of God only knows what, to carry temporarily, I always relive that scene.

As we approached the eastern end of town, one of the funniest events I ever saw took place. One of our squad, whose name I can no longer remember, emerged from the door of a house yelling, "All clear!" Walking immediately behind him in tandem was a German soldier with his arms raised high. If the German had been a snake, it would have bit him. Our squad member was a large man with a big smiling face. He also had big broad shoulders, which was a good thing, as we never let him forget the incident.

By four thirty that afternoon Ockfen was entirely in American hands, and the Mine Platoon of the Antitank Company went to work. With the help of about ten German prisoner "volunteers," they put in minefields across all of the eastern approaches to town to prevent another counterattack by the panzers. The only things with which we still had to contend were a heavy volume of fire from the pillboxes on the high ground to the southeast and enemy snipers beyond the town.

Our squad spent that night in one of the houses, and I slept on the floor. If there were any beds in the place, the noncoms got them. Before we got to sleep we received word that in the platoon command post Platoon Sergeant Lee had accidentally shot Lieutenant Ike in the leg with a German pistol. A lot of the men had pistols they had picked up, such as Lugers, Mausers, and a big affair we called a P-38. The trouble was the men were always playing around with them, and they would occasionally go off. Over a period of time we had several casualties from these accidental shootings.

Humor was sometimes rough, as you had to find it where you could. We got to joking about how Sergeant Lee and Lieutenant Ike had probably drawn straws to see who would get to get off the line. Lee lost so he had to stay, and Ike got to go into the evacuation mill. Of course, we all knew it was accidental, but if I entertained any small doubt it was soon to be dispelled that very night.

As I lay on the floor in the darkness, I wanted to get away from this nightmare with all my heart and soul. The affair in the platoon CP had caused me to think about accidents. I placed the muzzle of my rifle, which had been lying close to me, on my combat boot. I lightly fingered the trigger, being careful not to take up the trigger squeeze, and contemplated on how much of my foot I could blow off and not be a cripple for the rest of my life. One big problem would be in explaining the accident to people back home. What would I say later to my grandchildren when they questioned me?

"Granddaddy, how did you happen to shoot off your own toes during the war?" To which I would reply, "Grandson, that's a good question. Give me a minute and I'll give you an answer. Oh yes, it was like this. One day as I was standing with my rifle pointed down, a potato bug started to walk across in front of my foot. I jabbed at it with the muzzle but missed, striking my toes, and the jar set off a shot."

I jerked my hand away from the trigger. There was no way I could do it. I decided right then and there that I'd just have to let the Germans do it for me.

The next day, with most of the heat off of us momentarily, an infantryman's mind turned toward food. There was a large kitchen stove in the house, maybe a wood- or coal-burning type, I don't remember. At any rate, several of the men in the squad knew how to cook, so all we needed were the raw materials. One thing for sure, we had plenty of eggs. It was fun that morning, with everybody rummaging around through nearby houses to see what we could come up with for our noonday dinner. Several chickens, of course, lost their lives for a good cause.

It was then that I recalled the burgomaster's house with its wine cellar, and though I was not a wine fancier, I figured that some wine would add that certain touch to the dinner. Pat O'Connell and I walked down the street to the house, and much to our surprise we found it nothing but a smoldering pile of rubble. I thought how nice it was that we hadn't spent the night there. We had heard the German artillery coming in while we were sleeping, but unless it hit very close, you got blasé about that sort of thing. It's possible the Germans had the coordinates of the large house and assumed that perhaps some headquarters group would use it. I don't know if it was the same house or not, but the regimental book says that three staff officers were wounded that night by a direct hit on the battalion CP.

Pat and I tried to poke around through the smoldering debris to find the entrance to the cellar but had to give it up as it was too hot to handle.

When the food was finally prepared, about eight or nine of us gathered around a table. Our squad would always start off with twelve men when the replacements came in, but after a few days of chipping away, we'd be reduced in number. Someone said grace, and we dove into the vittles. This was the only home-cooked meal I had in the army, and I think it is the one that means the most to me in memory. Despite the unreal setting in which we had been placed, here we were like human beings sitting down to a family dinner.

Chapter Seven

It was a good thing we had a big hot home-cooked meal under our belts, because rest time was over, and that night we moved up on the hill north of Ockfen for outposting duties. We dug in, and I was sent on a lateral patrol to contact Company G, which had previously set up spread-out positions to the north. We accomplished this in the dark, although we worried about Company G shooting at us before bothering to challenge and hear the password. The Germans had lost Ockfen, and a small part of the hills to the north and south, but most of the real estate still belonged to them, and you didn't have to go very far to prove it.

That night and the next day, about half of Company F moved north along the riverside railroad track to attack the pillboxes in that area that were still giving trouble. Though facing stiff resistance, they finally met with success, and at least part of them rested the night of February 25 in or around one of the largest captured boxes. About nine thirty that night a large German infantry counterattack drove many of them into the box, where they were trapped and forced to surrender.

Around midnight, on the hill, the grapevine brought us the news of the trapped GIs. Several of us had gotten together in one large hole and were talking over the situation. One of our group was Blackie Grenier. Though he had come along with me in the first big batch of replacements, he already was almost an institution in the battalion. I'd say he was in his late thirties and couldn't have been much, if any, over five feet in height. How he passed the height requirement for getting into the army I'll never know, but I bet he browbeat somebody into letting him in.

Despite his size, part of him was as tough as nails. He had a very dark complexion and was from Chicago, maybe a tough part of the city. A real first name of "Abelard" probably hadn't hurt either in the early years of the toughening-up process. The other part of Blackie was very warm, friendly, and outgoing. My acquaintances beyond my own platoon were very few, but at such times as we would march by other platoons in our company or other companies in our battalion, we could hear shouts of "Hey, Blackie," and see a lot of arm waving. He had been promoted to buck sergeant and made assistant squad leader, and on a number of occasions he would talk to me as an old experienced hand at life, giving me encouragement. When I later told Mary Jo about him, because of his unusual nickname and size, looks, and personality, she believed she remembered dancing with him at a Red Cross–sponsored dance at Ft. Knox.

On this particular night, Blackie was trying to get us to go as a group to the new lieutenant and urge him to let the platoon go to the rescue of the trapped Company F members. This was the kind of guy he was. However, his following was not merely sparse, it was nonexistent. The others, including myself, were not eager for "beyond the call of duty," figuring that if they needed us, they would let us know.

As it turned out, the other half of Company F was recalled from Ockfen for the rescue attempt, but they were unable to break through the fire of a large number of machine guns set up by the Germans. Around two o'clock in the morning the Germans placed a large demolition charge in one of the embrasures of the pillbox. There was a terrific explosion followed by cries and groans of agony. Those Americans who lived soon surrendered, and those of Company F who could, withdrew.

The next day the Third Platoon of our company, supported by a solitary tank that had managed to make it across the river, was ordered to cover the withdrawal of the forty-eight men of Company F who were still pinned down and virtually cut off. This proved almost impossible when the one tank became the target of every enemy weapon in the vicinity. When the tank commander was wounded and crawled out through the hatch, the tank stopped firing. At this time an infantryman from our Third Platoon, Technician Fifth Grade Paul E. Ramsey, dashed to the tank, administered first aid to the tank commander, mounted the tank, and literally took charge of the battle, directing the fire of the tank's guns and using the tank's radio to give the battalion command post a clear and concise picture of the situation.

With the help of the tank's guns, the remainder of Company F and our Third Platoon was able to withdraw. Only a handful of men was left in the Third Platoon, including the mortally wounded platoon leader, Lieutenant Dyrlund. Our battalion commander, Lieutenant Colonel Martin, who had been directing the attack from a forward trench, was also wounded and evacuated, and command of the battalion now passed to the executive officer, Major Dossenbach. For his part in the action, Technician Fifth Grade Paul Ramsey was later awarded the Distinguished Service Cross.

For about a week after Ockfen we moved north into various positions up and down the huge hills on the east side of the Saar, digging foxholes all the way. Outside the one good meal in Ockfen, we lived off the K rations we carried in cardboard boxes in our packs. They weren't much, but they were better than starving. What few supplies the regiment received were brought across the river by assault boats and moved to the companies by carrying parties. Every attempt by the engineers to erect a bridge met with failure and heavy casualties. The German artillery and continuous rain of machine gun fire would puncture pontoons and riddle bridge-building equipment as fast as our men could haul it to the river.

When the supplies completely stopped coming, I remember one day sitting in my foxhole and eating part of a small can of cheese. I had cut out about a third of it, figuring I would eke out two more meals from the remainder.

Someone should write an "Ode to the Foxhole." Its very existence is a miracle of creation—a constant fight against sometimes soft, but oftentimes hard and rocky, soil. To attack the earth with our little trench shovels was like pitting a toothpick in battle against a block of granite as often as two or three times a day, with the toothpick always winning out. It's all I can do now to dig a hole to plant a bush for Mary Jo's garden. The difference lies, of course, in the motivation. All it took was the memory of a shell crashing and exploding within close range to fill the digger with the ferocity of one possessed by a demon. When done, the foxhole was your home, if only for a few hours, and you deeply appreciated the safety that it provided.

Honorable mention should also be accorded to the steel helmet. It, of course, had utilitarian values. It wasn't thick enough to stop direct shrapnel or a bullet, but it could redirect a glancing blow or stop a spent bit of shrapnel. You could sit on the rounded part of it fairly comfortably if weather and safety permitted. In a foxhole it was great for bailing out water or for using as a urinal if it wasn't safe to step out to the gents' room.

The psychological value of the helmet, however, was beyond estimation. It was symbolic of a protective shield around you. I'd like to find my old steel helmet to see if my fingernails carved any grooves along the sides where I pulled down so hard on it while in a foxhole. I think the only reason I couldn't get it on any further was that I couldn't get it past my shoulders.

On a clear day the view of the Saar River basin from atop one of the huge rounded hills was majestic. Sometimes you could pick up the fire of an American artillery piece miles to the west, and watch the little black dot of a shell traverse its way across the blue sky. At other times you could clearly see a line of German soldiers changing position on a distant hill. I wondered if they were just like us, doing what they had to do because they really had no choice.

The regiment slowly moved north along the Saar, clearing pillboxes and German defenses as it went. On the morning of March 1, my company was dug in on the hill overlooking Wiltingen, waiting for orders to take the town and surrounding pillboxes. Sometimes the Germans would have a pillbox in a town disguised as a house, with a range of fire down the key streets.

Someone from supply began handing out beehive and satchel charges, and, lucky me, I was given one of each. I was told that the others would fire into the embrasures of the pillbox, bottling it up, while I was to run up to the door of the box and blow it open by setting off the charges. There was just one catch. Looking them over as hard as I could, I couldn't figure out how to set them off. I certainly didn't recall learning anything about them in basic training, unless they came along during one of my sleep jobs, and I was too young, dumb, and embarrassed to seek out someone who knew and get proper instructions from them.

The American Psychological Warfare personnel on the west side of the river began blasting surrender orders over their loudspeakers to the people of Wiltingen. They informed the inhabitants of the town and neighboring pillboxes that their situation was hopeless, that an American armored division had encircled their rear and cut off all lines of supply (I think they lied), and that they had ten minutes to think it over and start waving white flags of some sort as signs of surrender. If they failed to do this, they were told that the town would be blasted into rubble.

The broadcast was in both German and English, and during that ten-minute wait, I prayed and I prayed and I prayed like I had never prayed before that the Germans would surrender, as I sure didn't want to have to try to use those charges. The Lord answered my prayers, and before long, white cloths were waving all over the place. Someone took the charges, and that was the last time I was ever given any, thank God!

The memory of that experience was indelible. On occasion through the years, in my nightmares, I have run up to a pillbox under the cover of rifle, Browning automatic rifle, and machine gun fire, carrying those damn beehive and satchel charges. I lay them by the door of the box and look them over and over and over, trying to figure out how to work them, even kicking them in disgust. Sometimes a German looks out through the peephole in the door then opens the door and shoots me with a pistol.

I received some solace recently when I happened to notice in the regimental book that on February 24, Company F had given their new replacements on-the-spot training on how to work the satchel charges and beehives. I didn't think we had gotten it in basic training! I have now vowed that sometime before my bones are laid to rest, I'm going to an armory or somewhere and learn how the charges operate, so my bones can rest in peace.

As the white flags of surrender began to wave, Company E moved into the southern part of Wiltingen. We took many prisoners, but one in particular was extremely interesting. We had stopped momentarily at the railroad station, where we ran into a young German soldier who had evidently been serving as some kind of a station attendant. He couldn't have been over nineteen or twenty, was very intelligent and friendly, and spoke excellent English. As age often seeks its own level, I and several of the other teenage members of our squad engaged in friendly conversation with him. He wasn't a Nazi fanatic but appeared to be somewhat bookish and wore glasses. There was no question in his mind but that this was merely a temporary setback and Adolf Hitler would soon rally his legions and drive the Allies back into the sea. The discussion grew into a philosophical debate, and like a group of schoolboys, we presented our opposing ideologies of democracy and socialism. We soon had to leave and exchanged good-byes and wishes of good luck. We moved on through town to the still-occupied defenses to the north, and he was taken back with the prisoners. What a strange vignette to fall in the middle of a war. I wonder whatever happened to him.

Our battalion spent the next three days clearing out well over a hundred pillboxes to the north. In the process we moved up and down the large hills in the area. Fortunately, not all of the boxes were occupied. If General Von Runstedt had fully manned every box, we'd be over there yet picking away at them, as they were so placed that the guns of one covered the blind spots of the other.

We also now had the advantage of some tank support from the Tenth Armored Division, whose tanks had finally been able to cross the Saar much farther to the south and work their way up to our area. It was an infantryman's delight when a tank could move right up to a box and fire a shell from its cannon directly into the embrasure. Though the boxes usually had several rooms, it must have been hell to have all that shrapnel ricocheting around inside. It usually took just one shell to have the survivors tumbling out to be taken prisoner. Our favorite loot from the interior of the pillboxes were a lemon-type soda and cigars.

On the first or second night in the hills south of Wiltingen, the weather turned very cold again and a stiff breeze came up. Pat O'Connell and I had dug in together in a two-man foxhole, and not having any blankets, we were miserable. At a short distance to our rear we could make out in the darkness the dim outline of what appeared to be an old wooden shed. With two great minds and but a single thought, we decided to get in the shed out of the wind and take turns sleeping, one of us lying down on the floor while the other watched out the door. It was totally dark inside, and as I lay down it felt like I was lying on a number of frozen corncobs. Upon closer examination, we realized the Germans had used the shed for an outhouse. Pat and I thought we had lost any fastidiousness, but you've got to draw the line somewhere, so we moved back to our foxhole.

We planned to sleep in shifts and spell each other every hour, but when it came my turn to watch, I was so cold I inadvertently fell asleep as a means of escape. The lieutenant rarely checked the line, but he did that night, and I was jarred awake by a foot kicking my helmet. The worst thing about a goof is to get caught, and I was caught. Thoughts flashed through my mind about how in the old days officers would shoot their men for dereliction of duty. Fortunately, all he did was chew us out, reminding us of the possibility of German counterattack by night. I suspect that if every soldier who goofed, on either the American or the German side, were shot for the trespass, it would have amounted to self-annihilation of the armies.

The next night, after a day spent in the usual clearing of pillboxes, we again dug in on a hill, facing a strong March wind and bitter cold. The foxholes were spread out badly, as we were covering a wide front. Pat and I were together again, and Ray Corser was in a one-man fox-hole to our left. Ray came over to visit us, I guess because misery loves company. To get some slight protection from the wind, the three of us sat down in the middle of a heavy weed patch nearby. It was at this point that there began a most unusual debate.

Each of us had his own idea about how to spend the balance of the night. Ray wanted to play it by the book and go back to our foxholes, feeling sure that we'd be checked on. Pat and I both believed the odds were against our being checked on two nights in a row, but that was the only thing on which we agreed. He wanted to stay in the weed patch, taking turns with one watching and the other two sleeping. On the other hand, I felt I had the best solution. About twenty-five feet to our right front was a knocked-out German tank. I suggested we climb on top, crawl through the hatch, and sleep inside. I contended this was the only real way to get out of the wind. Besides, there would have to be peepholes somewhere where one of us could always be looking out. I was so cold and frozen that the thought of possibly sharing the ac-commodations with some German corpses didn't bother me in the slightest.

The discussion evolved into one of those long-drawn-out things where no one was willing to give in. Finally realizing we were at a complete impasse, we agreed to settle it by drawing straws. In the darkness we broke off three lengths of weed stems. Pat pulled the long one, so we spent the night in the weed patch.

During this episode, the newspapers back in the United States were headlining the advances of Patton's mighty Third Army. On maps the front line was always indicated by a heavy black jagged line, creating the impression of solid steel. During the Korean and Vietnam wars, newspapers depicted the front lines in a similar way, attempting, I'm sure, to instill a national sense of security. For myself, I am never impressed, because whenever I think of a front line, I immediately get the picture of three boys sitting with their rifles in a weed patch in the dark, drawing straws.

At the crack of dawn the next morning Ray went back into his foxhole, and Pat and I went back to ours. A short time later they yelled from the bottom of the hill for us to come to breakfast, one foxhole at a time. The company kitchen had finally caught up with us, and we were going to get a hot meal. When it came time for Pat and me, we made the gross error of taking a shortcut along the crest of the hill instead of heading straight down. A German artillery observer evidently spotted us and sent an 88mm shell crashing close, which was soon followed by a whole battery firing for effect. As soon as we heard the first whistle of the first shell we both instinctively started running straight down the hill. By the time the volley hit we had nearly reached the bottom of the steep grade running full tilt; arriving at the base of the hill, we tumbled head over heels. After picking ourselves up we looked up the hill and then at each other and started laughing, which in itself seems a bit strange. I think what made it funny was seeing the great clouds of dust all over the top of the hill and realizing how great a distance we now were from the spot where we had created the havoc.

Though sharing the honors with Pat, this was the only time during the war that I was ever shelled by artillery as an individual; and since no one was hurt, I did feel honored. On numerous occasions, before and after, I was the recipient of shells but always on a very impersonal basis. The Germans would either shell prearranged targets, or where they thought we were, or where they observed us as a group, creating a feeling in me of just being a serial number in a vast mass of war machinery. But on this particular occasion I was fired on as an individual by an entire battery of enemy artillery, and for some odd and backhanded reason I felt important.

Chapter Eight

———————— On March 4, our battalion was relieved from line and given two days' rest in Wiltingen. The previous day the 376th Regiment had reverted to the control of the Ninety-fourth Division and was no longer attached to the Tenth Armored.

In Wiltingen, someone had rigged up some shower equipment in a large tent, and since we'd had no opportunity to bathe since leaving Veckring, France, on February 9, this was the first order of business. It's unbelievable the condition you can get in after three weeks of living in the mud and grime. Mary Jo now accuses me of smelling like a goat when I come home from playing golf. She's lucky she wasn't there at Wiltingen because I'm sure I smelled like a whole herd.

At this time the Siegfried Line had crumbled at all points, culminating with the capture of Trier by the First Battalion of our regiment. Perhaps the highest tribute paid to General Maloney and the whole Ninety-fourth Division, which operated south of Trier, came from the lips of the enemy. Reichsmarschall Hermann Goering, in an interrogation following his capture, stated: "When the first break in the Siegfried Line was made near Aachen, Der Fuhrer was very irritated. After that came the breakthrough near Trier, and that was wholly incomprehensible. We could not believe that these fortifications could be penetrated. The breakthrough near Trier was particularly depressing. That breakthrough and capture of the Remagen bridge were the two great catastrophes for the German cause."

While our regiment, the 376th, had been clearing out the Siegfried Line in the north toward Trier, the other two regiments, the 301st and the 302nd, had breached the southern parts of the Siegfried and moved some three or four miles to the east near the Ruwer. Once this small river was crossed, it appeared that the division would be moving fast as it had done after breaking through the Siegfried Switch Line on February 21. Only this time we would be driving not to the Saar but to the mighty Rhine.

Our two days of rest in Wiltingen were spent by our platoon in some kind of store building with several rooms. Gus Graham, who was still my squad leader, and the platoon guide, who ranked just above Gus, called me privately into a room. They told me that soon we might be having to move fast and emphasized how important it was that I keep up, because other men's lives depended on it. They spoke quietly and didn't blow it out of proportion, but if it had been anyone else other than Gus, I would have attempted to defend myself as I had done in front of Colonel McClune. It's true I'd had difficulty in climbing the hills since Ockfen, but God knows I had tried. On one occasion they had issued overcoats, and despite the cold, I had thrown mine away rather than be slowed down by the weight. I had thrown away my bandoliers, saving only the clips in my cartridge belt, and divested myself of all but two hand grenades, figuring it was better to arrive light in ammunition than not to arrive at all. I had scoured my pack to see what surplus and unnecessary articles I could discard. I had even tossed out a box of toothpicks. That was more of a sacrifice than you think, because you had to pick up every little bit extra you could from those skimpy K rations.

Since it was Gus who spoke to me, I said nothing of those things, as I would have gone to hell and back for Gus, or at least would have tried. I simply told him that I would do my best. As it turned out, the situation soon took care of itself. With the rest in Wiltingen, the weather turning warmer, and with the innate resilience of an eighteen-year-old, I started to regain a measure of my previous strength as my chest began to slowly clear. I was also able to resume wearing my full equipment.

A time of rest meant, of course, that men would sit around on the floor in small groups shooting the breeze. If the new replacements were around, I would show them my pictures, and they would show me theirs. I always liked to hang back on showing Mary Jo's picture where she looked like a movie star. Then, as the coup de grâce, I'd display it amid the aaahs and ooohs.

Mostly, however, I liked to sit back and listen to the older men talk. A few of them had volunteered instead of being drafted, and did they gripe! It was one thing to be in this mess because you had no other choice, but to have done it to yourself was a bitter pill to swallow. I got into a group that included my savior, the man who had exposed himself to fire to pull me into the trench at Ockfen. I stared at him and listened to him talk. He was around thirty, and very human, telling how in relations with his girlfriend nothing made him more angry than to reach a climax before he was ready. When the subject got around to foxhole religion, he said he didn't pray when things got tight, because when things were going good, he didn't go to church or pray, and he didn't feel it was right to pray only when he was in trouble.

I couldn't help but wonder, had the tables been reversed, would I, a so-called Christian, have exposed myself to fire for him? This conversation made a strong impression on me, and though I am a strong proponent of the church and church attendance, I put no credence in any talk of damnation for the unchurched or those who do not attend church. For some reason I failed to retain his name, but his face, which like so many others soon disappeared to be replaced by a replacement, I will always remember.

A time of rest is also a time when the mail clerk catches up with you, and I'm sure the poor fellow must have felt besieged with everybody ganging up on him. March 4, I wrote Mary Jo: "Dear Jo, Well, honey, I've gotten a chance to drop you another letter. I got your February 22 letter today. I think I could write a volume on what your letters mean to me, Jo, but I'll settle in saying that there have been times when I don't think I would have made it without them. I believe I've gotten all your January letters (the 5, 7, 15, 19, 25, and 27). I've taken them out many times in my foxhole and reread them. So you see, honey, I'm really depending on you for my morale.

"I haven't received your valentine yet, but I am anxiously awaiting it. I also haven't received those snapshots you seemed so worried about. You wouldn't be so worried if I could have taken some pictures of myself the last few weeks. A soldier looks pretty grim after being in foxholes a couple of weeks without washing or shaving. I bet the De-Molay boys wouldn't know me, all covered with mud and loaded down with my rifle, bayonet, grenade launcher, cartridge belt, three bandoliers, canteen, pack, and hand grenades hanging all over me. Quite a change from the days I used to doll up in my tux several times a week, don't you think?

"You asked if you had time to get frightened over here. Believe me, Jo, there's no time required. It only takes about a tenth of a second for a gray hair to start working its way up.

"I gather from your last letter that your visiting me has caused some confusion. For myself, it doesn't matter what other people think just so that *we* understand each other. You hit the nail on the head when you said we have such a 'comfortable relationship.' I feel that way too. I guess it would be sorta hard to explain the relationship to someone else, but I understand it and I know you do, too. It's something that comes directly from the heart with no strings attached. If I could be with you there'd be a million things I could say that I don't know how to put on paper.

"Well, Jo, what do you think of this letter? I've just reread what I've written thus far and had to chuckle because they sure don't pan out like they used to. I try to sound my old gay self but I guess it's just not there. Darling, I might as well be frank with you. I'm living in a different world now—a world in which I find it very hard to be cheerful. So please bear with me until this mess is over. I can assure you that once it is over and I can get back to my old way of life I'll be my same ole self.

"You wondered if I thought of that last night much. Believe me, Jo, I've relived every minute of it time, time, and again. Well, I'd better wind this up. This is all for awhile from a GI who loves you very much. Dickie."

Mary Jo had written me: "Dear Dick, hi there, honeychile. I wrote you those first three words about an hour ago. Then mother and Jackie came into the bedroom to talk to me. After a long discussion I had to wrestle around with Jackie awhile to make him go to bed. He is really strong, but I manage to hold my own. I know my girl friends with brothers wouldn't be able to understand how I enjoy dancing around with Jackie, and acting crazy, but you know how close our family is, and I want to keep it that way. If I shut Jackie out of my conversation and thoughts just because he's younger and a 'kid brother in school,' he'd be crushed. Besides, I just love that kid so much it hurts. If he didn't like to be with me, I'd be an unhappy gal.

"Dickie-boy, I think of you constantly, and worry about you. Tonight I had gone to bed early because I was a 'Melancholy Baby' for sure. I could just see in my mind all the things that I know might very easily happen to you, and it was too much for me. I tried to escape my thoughts with sleep, but I wasn't doing such a good job. Mother and Jackie knew what was wrong, so they came in to cheer me up. Then I got up to listen to this Jazz Concert and finish my letter to you. I know that worrying doesn't do anyone any good, and that my vivid imagination just makes matters worse, but I can't help it.

"Dickie, honey, I know you don't think about religion very often, so when I talk about praying for your safety, it probably doesn't matter much to you whether I do or don't. I have faith, though, darling, and I don't miss a night. You will come back. I know that, even when I find myself worrying.

"I'll be thinking of you, wherever you are, honey, no matter where I am or what I'm doing. And each night I'll be sending a prayer and a kiss. Goodnight, and all my love, Mary Jo."

I did care about her prayers, however, very much, and later told her so. I also wrote: "Believe me, Jo, there are no atheists in foxholes. Remember the Sunday we went to church together? I enjoyed it more than I admitted." War has a way of ripping your soul wide open, turning it inside out, and ravaging it with the direst of stresses. Without a belief in God, rationality would be almost impossible.

I had learned a fear of death the summer I was fifteen when, after being covered with ticks from a fishing trip to Montauk State Park, I came down with Rocky Mountain Spotted Fever. In those days, before any serum, only about one in ten people afflicted lived. After the fever subsided, Doc Vaughn told me that only about one of ten survivors would be free of heart trouble for the rest of his or her life and that he wanted me to lie on my bed for sixty days and remain quiet. So I lay there fearfully counting my own pulse and praying to God, promising that if I pulled through without any heart trouble, I'd be such a different person. I pulled through in good shape, and then I proceeded to forget all about God, merrily going on my own way.

The next summer a trout-fishing stream about did me in. Jim Benjamin, Paul Williams, and I were caught in a flash flood at Bennett Spring State Park and had our pictures on the front page of the *Kansas City Star*. It was because of our own stupidity that we were washed away. Despite the fact that cars and trailers were being swept downstream before our eyes, we made trip after trip to our campsite to move our equipment to higher ground. I would have never waded out for that last trip to rescue the tent if I had not been a Boy Scout Junior Life Saver. I had absolutely no fear of water, figuring that nothing could ever happen to me. As the rising water began to inch us off our feet, Jim Benjamin, who later became a lawyer, said, "Let's keep calm, boys!" Unfortunately, it was too late for calmness as the water picked us up and swept us away. Paul was able to hang onto some logs and was carried several miles down the Niangua River before being able to reach the bank. Jim and I managed to stay in the park by grabbing some trees as we sailed by. The tree I climbed was a small one, and I feared it would be carried away as the stream spread out into a roaring rampage a quarter of a mile wide. As if by a miracle, logs began to pile up against two larger trees immediately upstream of my position, forming a dam that threw the water on both sides around me.

Boats from Branwell's Camp on the north and ones from the south attempted to rescue us, but they were turned over as soon as they were launched. Spending several hours hanging on for dear life in the fork of this little tree, barely above water, gave me plenty of time to once again seek out the Lord. The only religious song I could think of was "Silent Night," and knowing only the first verse, I sang that over and over again. Guess where my thoughts return at Christmastime when I hear "Silent Night."

I also prayed and prayed to God that if I could be delivered, I'd be such a different person. God delivered us all right, through the auspices of the Missouri State Police, who steered a huge launch slowly upstream, tied it to a large tree, then let it float downstream to rescue first Jim and then me. A cheering crowd on the south bank welcomed us, and the sheriff's deputies drove us to the hospital in Lebanon.

As I became more scientifically oriented in my last two years of high school and first year in junior college, I began thinking there must be a scientific cause and answer for everything, even though the answer might never be uncovered. Within this structure there was little need for any conception of a deity. At least outwardly I was proclaiming myself to be an atheist and enjoyed arguing along these lines with my optometrist, Dr. Littlefield, who was a devout Christian. It was at this stage of my development that Mary Jo had picked up my lack of feeling for religion.

By the time I reached the front lines, however, my third cycle of religious fervor was beginning to come around. I had been baptized not only with artillery, but also with foxhole religion, at least enough to keep praying most of the time for my skin. My approach was a far cry from the honesty of the man who had pulled me into the trench. Why is it that so many of us wait until we are in trouble before seeking God?

It was at Wiltingen that I experienced the greatest emotional roller coaster of my life. By the evening of March 4, the grapevine had brought the wonderful news that the entire Ninety-fourth Division was going to be relieved by the Twenty-sixth Division and that we would go back for ten days of rest in Luxembourg. By the next day the regiment was waiting only for the order to pull back. For the Third Battalion the order actually did come through, and they quickly moved into Dudelange, Luxembourg. Our battalion had sent an advance party, including a couple of men from our platoon, in order to make housing arrangements. The very name of Luxembourg sounded charming and exciting, a small European country I had often looked at on the world history maps I pored over as a child. I had no idea what delights would be in store for me. Any place that would get me off the front line would be heaven, but to go to Luxembourg was beyond my wildest imagination.

Excitement ran high for everyone that day, as we looked forward to being relieved. Early that night we were ordered to get on our equipment and move out to Luxembourg. It's the only time I ever remember not minding having to put on all the equipment. As we marched north through town, spirits ran high, and everybody was laughing and joking. We assumed we were going north along the river, in the direction of Trier, in order to cross the Saar at some point and head west into Luxembourg.

At a road junction, for some reason, the column made a wrong turn and headed east in the darkness toward the sound of the guns at the front. As we continued toward the front, we kept talking among ourselves as to what could possibly be the explanation. Finally we received word from our platoon leader, Lieutenant Brusher, that an emergency had developed and that there would be a change of plans. To the east the 301st and 302nd Regiments were in trouble. The German Sixth SS Mountain Division had attacked the division front and breached it at several points. The Germans were all twenty-three to twenty-five years of age. They had had three years of combat experience, were in good physical condition, and possessed high morale. Repeatedly, they had fought with the fanaticism peculiar to SS troops.

A large number of the German storm troopers had infiltrated in the darkness and formed a pocket atop an open hill south of Pellingen. The First and Second Battalions of the 376th were the only units immediately available to counter this new threat. The division relief was canceled, and our Third Battalion was recalled from its very brief rest in Luxembourg. This news brought silence to the platoon, and I felt all torn up inside.

We got as far as Oberemmel that night, digging in along the main road near the town. We dug two-man foxholes close together and no sooner had settled in them than we received the usual "incoming mail." My head was below the surface of the ground, so I didn't think too much about it, but evidently one hit at just the wrong time. The next morning at dawn Pat and I heard activity near the foxhole to our right and looked in time to see several men lifting Blackie's body onto a stretcher. They covered him up, and all we could see were his boots as they took him away.

We learned later that during the shelling he had had a cramp in his leg, stood up in the foxhole, and had the top half of his head blown off. The young replacement, for whom it was the first night at the front, spent the night with Blackie, frozen in shock, and had to be evacuated. I'll never forget that morning. Why is it the brave are carried off?

All during the war, whenever we had to pass where other units had been before, they were always good about covering up the American dead if there hadn't been time to remove the bodies. Usually they covered each man with a poncho, raincoat, or overcoat, but as a rule, the boots would be sticking out. The Germans would be left exposed where they fell, sometimes in piles if artillery had caught a bunch of them. To see dead German soldiers transcribed itself in the mind to read that the war would be over just that much sooner. To see the lifeless forms of the American dead, however, covered all except for their boots, was a different matter entirely. There was a sickening, sinking feeling in the pit of my stomach, followed by a flood of joy that I was still alive and could move and flex my muscles. Later came a feeling of guilt over the joy I had felt.

On the first night after leaving Oberemmel we dug one-man foxholes in near-total darkness under a heavily overcast sky. Our position was along the base of an earth shelf, which stood several feet above us. We were unaware that on the shelf a .50-caliber heavy machine gun had taken a position prior to our arrival. It had to have come from one of the weapons companies, as our weapons platoon carried only the lighter .30 caliber.

At the first crack of dawn the machine gun opened up. Since I knew nothing of its existence the thunderous roar sent a traumatic message that a machine gun directly over my head was firing straight down into my foxhole. Then, recovering from the shock, I realized that the target was German infantry advancing out of the woods to our front. We joined fire with the machine gun and continued firing until the Germans retreated into the woods, leaving behind their dead and wounded.

During the next several days, the First Battalion, with tank support, took the brunt of eliminating the German pocket south of Pellingen, while our battalion passed through to plug the gap in the ruptured line of the Third Battalion, 302nd, and thus stabilize the division front. As we moved into Obersehr dead German soldiers were strewn everywhere, some, like Blackie, with the top halves of their heads blown off by artillery, as if watermelons had been sliced in two.

Moving into Lampaden late at night, we again dug one-man foxholes. It was so dark you couldn't see your hand in front of your face. At dawn a member of our platoon, a tall young man with glasses, found that he had dug in next to a dead German whose hand was practically hanging into his foxhole. We all got a big laugh out of this.

Later in the morning I had nothing to laugh about. I had cheated on digging the night before and lay horizontally in a large rectangular hole that had probably been used by the Germans for a mortar position. It was here that I received my worst shelling. A whole barrage came in right on top of us. I bounced up and down like a rubber ball, so high sometimes that I think if the timing had been right I would have been cut to ribbons by the shrapnel, as I was suspended in midair above the surface of the ground. At no other time had I ever experienced this particular sound of the relentless incoming whine of the shells. It was as if a giant magnet were drawing them toward me as a target.

When the shelling ceased, the dust clouds billowed all around. Soon someone called the squad to collect in a nearby house. As I tried to light a cigarette, my hand was shaking so badly that someone had to light it for me. Hot food or stew was passed out for our canteen cups, and I remember my spoon banging and rattling against the insides, almost out of control. My nerves had temporarily disintegrated. The fact that for a number of years I would instinctively hit the deck at the sound of a Fourth of July rocket, I attribute in no small part to this shelling at Lampaden.

Chapter Nine

By March 9, the division front was more or less stabilized along the Ruwer River. By the 12th, things had quieted enough that our company was given several days' rest in Lampaden, although we were on the alert and subject to patrol and outposting duty. The house in which our squad was located was quite comfortable, despite the fact that we had to sleep on the floor. The weather had turned much warmer. To sleep on a floor was a luxury compared to being in a foxhole.

Replacements came in droves, our squad alone taking six to bring it up to full strength, or twelve. In one month I'd be nineteen, and here they were sending up these green eighteen-and-a-half-year-old kids! By now, in terms of service, I was one of the oldest men in the platoon, with most of the other old members moving into positions of authority. Gus Graham had moved up to platoon guide while Ben Siegel had become squad leader and Ray Corser his assistant. I had no camera, but there were some who did, and this became a time of great picture taking. Most of the pictures I have come from this period. In one, Chernak, who was always cutting up, had donned a German officer's cap and field glasses and was standing with the raised stiff arm of a Nazi salute while Gus Graham and several others held him at bay with their rifles.

It was also, of course, a time for the receiving and writing of letters. I had gotten some news about some of the old gang, and I passed it along to Mary Jo: "Scottie passed his physical at Leavenworth several weeks ago. I just got a letter from him and he says he believes he will

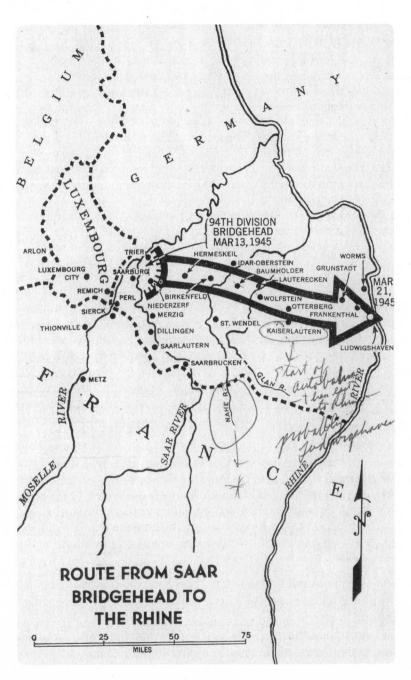

ROUTE FROM SAAR BRIDGEHEAD TO THE RHINE

Route from Saar bridgehead to the Rhine

volunteer for immediate induction. I'm afraid he had gotten a rosy picture of this whole mess. Ted has finished basic training and went to Oregon to see his folks. Helen went there to see him. I imagine he is overseas by now. Modlin was in a rest camp in Belgium about a month ago, but I guess he's right in the middle of that push up there by now. Johnny Middleton was wounded down in the South Pacific, but they patched him up and he is back in action again."

I then turned to matters of a much more personal nature.

"Jo, I'm sorta at a loss as to how to say the million things I want to. Since my letter to you last week I've received six or eight more of your letters. I can't describe the way they have affected me. Darling, I could be compared to a man who married a girl because he loved her with all his heart, and then after several years he finds he loves her all the more when he didn't think it possible. I love you and have but one intention concerning you when I get back. I've never been quite this frank, have I, Jo? I had a reason and probably ought to be kicked for doing it now. It isn't fair to you, honey. More than anything in the world I don't want to hurt you if something should happen to me. I hope I don't sound morbid or pessimistic because I'm not. God knows I want to come back so bad I can't see straight, as there is so much to come back to."

I had received her February 27 letter and she wrote: "Remember that picnic in Swope Park when you made good on your threat to spank me? I don't even think I'd mind that habit you acquired this last time we were together, of giving me a gentle spank every time I got in the car, if it meant that we would go out in the dear old thing again. I'd give anything I possess to be able to live over New Year's Eve. I relive it in mind constantly. I remember when at four o'clock in the morning we danced some more—I had on my black dress and pink bedroom slippers—and you stopped dancing and we stood still and you said 'If everything stayed just as it is right now, I'd be content for the rest of my life.'"

At the same time I was writing Mary Jo from Lampaden, she was writing me a letter I was to receive later: "Honey, the newspapers are calling Patton's victories Germany's major defeat of the war. Maybe you boys will be the first to be sent home when the war with Germany is over. I hope so—gosh, I hope so. The 94th Division has been in the newscasts for the past several nights. You know I'm praying for you, honey. I'd give twenty years of my life if it would insure twenty more minutes for you. And I'm not being dramatic. I mean it from the bottom of my heart."

On March 15, our regiment began its big push to the Rhine. It was but a small part of a massive operation, which included fourteen divisions of the Seventh Army and the Twentieth Corps of Patton's Third Army. The Twentieth Corps was made up of four divisions, one of which was our Ninety-fourth.

Our other two regiments, the 301st and 302nd, initiated the drive on March 13, successfully crossing the small Ruwer River, and the next day they breached the German lines on the east side. The 376th lay in motorized reserve, waiting to exploit a breakthrough anywhere along the division front. On the 15th we boarded trucks and moved out, feeling like it was really something for infantry not to have to be on foot. The fun didn't last long, because as soon as our battalion reached Heddert we were on foot again. We moved into one small town after another during the next few days, meeting with only light resistance.

To expedite matters and prevent the necessity of calling for artillery before going into a town, the officers came up with a real nifty idea. The idea was for two men to go into the town first, and if nobody opened up on them, they would wave the others in. I lucked out for several towns, but then they picked Pat and me to go in while the rest of the platoon waited about a quarter of a mile from the first houses. Pat and I advanced, one on either side of the road, both of us keeping an eye on the ditch. We kept hoping that if they were going to open up, they'd do it before we ran out of ditch. Thankfully, nothing happened, but by the time we got into town we were sweating like we had been in a Turkish bath.

We went into one of the first houses, and lo and behold, in it were several elderly Germans. These were the first German civilians with whom we had ever come face to face. With the exception of Wiltingen, whose civilians had been kept separated from us, all other towns had been vacated.

As we pointed our rifles at them, they just about went to pieces. For one cruel moment the feeling of power that I had experienced with the machine gun nest prisoners at Thorner Woods swept over me. However, I soon realized they were only frightened human beings and lowered my rifle. As best they could they told us, mostly with sign language, that the German soldiers had abandoned the town, so we immediately went outside and waved in the platoon.

We were moving extremely fast for infantry, but for a change, I was almost leading the pack. The rest at Lampaden and the current sunshine had finished off the chest congestion that had so long enervated me. I had a spring to my step and a hope in my heart that, with the German army beginning to reel, the war might be over before my number came up.

Being one of the oldest members in terms of service, I noticed that the new replacements looked up to me for guidance, as I had looked to others in the past. I took them under my wing, cautioning them to always keep a sharp lookout for some kind of indentation in the ground to dive into at the first split-second whistle of an incoming shell. I also stressed the importance of digging in superfast whenever we stopped, in order to be ready for any shelling. To learn things of this nature by experience might well be to learn too late.

After several days, what had been a fairly well ordered German retreat became a rout, and on our part, the attack became an endurance contest. The regiment pursued the retreating enemy as rapidly as possible, using leapfrogging battalions. By March 19, the regiment had become almost completely motorized with troops climbing down only to rest or to eliminate the infrequent resistance. In most towns we were greeted by white sheets, shirts, and towels hanging from every window indicating the villagers' unwillingness to follow Hitler's command to resist the invaders unto death.

The scenery throughout most of the advance was typical of the rural areas of southern Germany. The frequent hills were covered with aromatic pine forests so thick with trees that they were dark and cool despite the brightest sunshine. Clear bubbling streams ran down the hills into wide lovely valleys, all intensively cultivated. The quaint little towns looked like illustrations from Grimm's fairy tales.

The weather being clear with perfect visibility, the sky filled with fleets of American bombers, soon to wreak havoc on the long columns of German troops, equipment, and supplies frantically trying to reach the comparative safety of the east bank of the Rhine. To be a part of this vast panorama, moving rapidly in trucks, with armadas of planes overhead, was a once-in-a-lifetime experience. For the first time, I felt I was part of something world-shaking, and there was no doubt in my mind about the ability of the Allies to crush the German armies.

Before long we saw the handiwork of the United States Army Air Force. They had had a field day bombing the closely packed German convoys. Due to the acute shortage of gasoline in Germany, almost all of the Wehrmacht vehicles had been horse-drawn. Many of the horses had been killed, and their corpses blocked the road. Many demolished trucks and wagons were still burning; others were overturned, their contents spilled along the roadside. Knocked-out tanks, kitchens, ambulances, ammunition carts, and field pieces were a common sight.

German soldiers began to emerge from the woods, their arms raised in surrender. At first they came by twos and threes, then by the hundreds, and then by the thousands, until the roads were packed with shuffling green-clad figures. No guards were assigned. The willing prisoners were merely ordered to continue marching to the west, where they were eventually picked up by POW teams, who herded them into already overcrowded enclosures. To see thousands of German prisoners only magnified my confidence of an imminent Allied victory. My confidence was a bit premature.

For a short time we rode on the Autobahn that stretched from Kaiserslautern to the metropolis of Ludwigshafen on the Rhine. I supposed there were some freeways on the American east and west coasts, but having never seen any in the Kansas City area, I found it exciting to ride down one side of the magnificent twin highways.

By March 21, our battalion had moved into Oggersheim to prepare for its role in the attack on Ludwigshafen. We had covered approximately one hundred miles in six days, but our swift pursuit of the Germans was over. Although we didn't yet know it, the high command had issued orders that the city was to be defended to the last man. Ludwigshafen, with a population of around one hundred fifty thousand, was the pride of the Saar Palatinate and home of Germany's greatest chemical plant, I. G. Farben Industrien. The city was ably defended by the German Ninth Flak Division, a veteran outfit that for years had made the skies over Ludwigshafen and other industrial cities a hell for RAF and USAAF bomber crews. Many of them had been deployed around the city as infantry troops, while the rest depressed their 88mm flak guns to zero elevation for use against attacking armor and personnel. Into the city had also drifted the remnants of many other battered German divisions, adding to the strength of the fanatical defenders already present.

Those elements of the American Twelfth Armored Division that were in the zone of the Ninety-fourth attempted to seize Ludwigshafen using the same headlong tactic that had won city after city in the drive to the east. Unfortunately, most of the tanks ended up as blackened, driverless hulls in front of the German 88s. Visibility from the gun positions was almost perfect. No one could make a move on the open ground in front of the city without being spotted. The Germans also had on hand boxcars full of 88mm ammunition.

In addition to the fact that we could count on very little tank support, there would be no artillery barrages to herald any attack we might make. The division's artillery battalions had arrived, but there was no ammunition train, as the trucks normally used for this purpose had been hauling us infantry boys. This meant the batteries had available only those rounds carried on the prime movers.

Oggersheim was a large suburb of Ludwigshafen with a sizable civilian population. We moved in at night, and for a short time our platoon stayed in a modern apartment building. Along with several others I was assigned to share a room on the second floor in which there were beds. I lay claim to a bed, dumped off my equipment, and figured I'd get a good night's sleep. I should have gone to bed, but I decided to explore the place and found a piano in one of the rooms downstairs. I was no great shakes as a piano player, but I had been the pianist for our Boy Scout band. I played some of my old favorites, including "Star Dust," very conscious of the fact that this was a weird setting for playing music.

I went upstairs to bed and had no sooner gone to sleep than someone informed me I would have to take a turn for guard duty outside. My post was in the alley behind the apartment building, looking east for any possible German patrol or movement. It was then I got one of those brilliant ideas that turns out to be a dud.

We had just recently been issued sleeping bags, and I had one in my pack. The night was very cold, so I removed the sleeping bag from my pack, unzipped it, then got into it while standing up. Using my left hand, which was outside the bag, I leaned my rifle against my body and shoved it securely into the pocket formed by the thumb and forefinger of my right hand, which was inside the bag. With my left hand I then zipped her up, leaving only my face exposed to the cold wind and my body leaning comfortably against the wall of a building. It was my intention at the first sound or the sight of any movement to quickly unzip the bag with my left hand and step out of it.

In about a half hour I did hear footsteps and immediately went into Plan A, which was to quickly unzip the zipper. But you know what always happens to zippers when you're in a big hurry to unzip them, particularly with one hand. Yanking with all my might, I just couldn't get it to work. I didn't dare use my right hand to hold the lower part of the zipper taut for fear my rifle would fall and clatter on the cobblestone alley. As the quiet footsteps approached I could make out the dim outlines of a German probe patrol. I was petrified. Standing in the dark shadows of the alley, I thought, "Dear God, don't let them see me!" Happily they passed on.

Of course, if they had seen me and stuck a bayonet in my stomach and pinned me to the wall, the telegram to my parents might have read: "We regret to inform you that your son was killed with a bayonet through his sleeping bag—while in a vertical position."

Shame kept me from reporting the matter at the time or even telling anyone about it later. After sixty years I guess it's safe now to report the incident. As the years have gone by I've grown to see the humor of it all. In war, when goofs are committed and someone is hurt it is tragic, but when no one is hurt it's funny. As far as I know no one was hurt.

Maybe I should have reported it: "Yes, sir, it was like this, Lieutenant. There's a German patrol out there that went that way. The reason they went that way was that at the time I happened to be standing in my zipped-up sleeping bag and it wouldn't unzip." With an incredulous look on his face, the lieutenant says, "You were standing in *what*?"

Someone else came to take over guard duty, and I returned to bed, where I had just settled down good when they rousted us out about two o'clock in the morning for an attack on the small suburb of Maudach. Our company, along with a heavy machine gun section from Company H, led the battalion into the town. By four thirty, Maudach was taken.

For the next twelve hours our squad was located in a small house overlooking the flat pool table–like ground of the Rhine valley. Besides time for a few hours of rest in the morning, we lay around on the floor close to the front door and visited like a family. Our number had gone from twelve to nine since the big push had started, with Pat, Komiske, and Beardsley being transferred to POW duty.

Our BAR man, one of the new replacements, had a camera, and we took a number of pictures of the squad. He was a fair-sized kid and so had been given the BAR, or Browning automatic rifle. My being small, that's the one thing they never gave me to carry. I'd never have made it if they had. There was one camera shot I'd give anything to have, and that was the one of a trio, with me in the middle and Lopez and Bergum on either side, all standing with our arms around one another's shoulders. The reason I would like to have it is that both Lopez and Bergum were killed by rifle fire the next day.

It was late in the morning when Trautwein, another of the new replacements, and I did a little exploring and witnessed what was, for me, the most heartrending sight of the war. We had climbed some rear steps to the top of a flat-roofed single-story building. From there we could look out over the flat ground toward another suburb about a half mile away. Around the top of the building was a sort of parapet, and from this vantage point we watched the playing of an unusual scene.

In a courtyard near some of the suburb's buildings an 88mm had been caught by American 105mm fire. The Germans had evidently been trying to move the cannon when our artillery spotted them. By now the 105s had zeroed in, and shell after shell was falling right on target. Despite this fact, group after group of Germans was sent out from the buildings in a futile attempt to save the field piece. As fast as one group was mowed down another took its place, the courtyard soon becoming littered with bodies. It would have taken a cruel soul to have enjoyed such a senseless, wanton waste of life, even if they were the enemy. It would have been virtually impossible for a situation of this nature to have occurred on the American side. I think this was one of the fundamental differences between the two armies.

I cannot imagine an American officer sending his men to certain death once the target had been zeroed in. Nor can I imagine an American soldier obeying such an order if it had been given. Recently, in Iraq, a unit refused to drive vehicles that had totally insufficient armor. Most were punished with something akin to KP duty. The sergeant in command was demoted one grade in rank. I'd rather be a live corporal than a dead sergeant.

Late in the afternoon, our company went to the assistance of Company F in clearing out the last of the enemy resistance in Rheingonheim, still another suburb of Ludwigshafen. Having completed the mission, we settled down in the town for the night.

At five thirty on the morning of March 23, our platoon, along with the Second, prepared to move against Mundenheim, the last suburb before Ludwigshafen proper, coming from the south. Our squad was on the extreme left of the two platoons and approximately fifty yards from the railroad tracks leading northeast into Mundenheim. We had about five hundred yards of open ground to cross but could see nothing in the dark as we filed through a large hole in a stone wall out onto the field. Once on the field we were put into extended spread formation and told to squat down and wait for orders to advance. I can only presume that the intention was for the two platoons to move out before dawn from this line of embarkation that had been set up on an open field.

The assumption on the part of the little guy in the platoons was that the area directly in front of us had been cleared by another company or battalion, or we wouldn't be parked out there in the open. We were no tacticians, but just about anybody would know that you would have to either cross at night, or if crossing by day, wait behind some kind of protection, then move out fast across the field, perhaps employing marching fire to prevent being pinned down. For whatever reason, the area to the front had not been cleared; dawn broke, and our two platoons were caught like fish in a barrel and soon decimated. In our squad alone, out of nine men, three were killed and four wounded.

As dawn broke, rifle fire followed by machine gun fire fell on us from the houses to the front. There was a moment when we could have broken for the rear and for the most part made it back safely; however, I'm sure that everyone was thinking, as I was, that in the very next instant surely someone would order us to charge the enemy emplacements. Everybody had hit the prone position, and since we were so spread out, we lost all visual contact.

Fortunately, I was toward the rear of the squad, and Trautwein was directly in front of me. There was a huge bomb crater several feet to our right. We moved over and slipped into the edge of it just a few inches, in order to present a low profile, yet still be able to see or hear any order to advance. However, Ben Siegel, the squad leader, for one, wasn't about to give orders to anyone; he lay with deep bullet grooves in both sides of his skull.

The artillery soon started to come in, and as if things weren't bad enough, besides the regular stuff they also started throwing some time fire that would explode twenty or thirty feet about the ground, preventing a prone position from being of any value. Then to turn the whole scene into a veritable Dante's inferno, the eight carloads of

88mm artillery ammunition on the railroad tracks to our immediate left were hit by shells and started to explode in a chain reaction, filling the air with jagged fragments of steel. Lopez and Bergum, who were scouts in front of Ben, were killed. I don't know in what manner. The BAR man behind Ben was shot through the groin. The young replacement to my right front, out of sight, was hit by shrapnel in the back, but it was the youngster to my left at the distance of some fifteen or twenty yards, well within my vision, who has been my eternal concern.

Clifford Tipton had joined us at Lampaden ten days before and had the makings of another Gus Graham or Blackie Grenier. He was one of the few who just couldn't wait to get into action. A short time after all hell had broken loose, he had been hit, I know not how. Later, he began to cry for his mother, perhaps dying by that time, perhaps not. By rights, with my seniority I should have been both his mother and his father, but I was neither. In a thousand nightmares since, I have braved the fire to drag him over to the bomb crater to administer first aid or prevent a possible second wound.

At the time, though, the thought never occurred to me, and if it had, it was not in my nature to play the part of hero. If it had been Pat over there, I like to think I would have done it, but for no one else. I believe the greatest guilt of all that arose later stemmed from the fact that the thought never occurred to me to call out to him to try to crawl over to the comparative security of the bomb crater. This would have cost me nothing in either time or safety, but by now I was the perfect infantry automaton, who, in the midst of a holocaust, had but the single thought that at any moment I would be called upon to charge the enemy.

I think it was from these feelings of guilt, as much as any other reason, that I felt called to take the training to become a part-time Methodist minister for nine years. I felt that in some way I could live his life, too, and make up for the things he would have done. This is a poor reason for becoming a minister, as it's tough enough trying to live one life. Besides, it creates the tendency to set impossible goals for yourself. I no longer wake up crying with guilt, as the mature man has long since realized that God has forgiven the eighteen-year-old boy. I only have a deep sense of sadness, wishing it had not happened.

In later years I was finally able to locate Ben Siegel and make telephone contact. I found out that he was a professor of English at Cal State Poly Tech at Claremont, California. Down through the years Ben, too, had been tormented by Tipton's loud cries for "Mama." I learned that when Tipton was first struck he was somehow thrown to his back so that his field pack pushed him up for a continual target. In fact, it was in raising himself and yelling at Tipton to turn over off his pack that Ben had been struck in the skull by bullets. This explained why in my nightmares Tipton had always appeared in high profile.

Ben also told me I had done the right thing by not attempting to drag Tipton to the bomb crater, as it would have been "near suicide." Perhaps it is out of a need for me to hear this that I call him periodically.

I did receive an order, but it was not the one I expected. From behind the wall to the rear I heard Ray Corser, the assistant squad leader, yell out. He motioned me back with his arm. I in turn yelled at Trautwein, pointed at Corser, and cried, "Let's go!" The machine gun fire had subsided for the moment, but intermittent rifle fire continued. We ran the gauntlet for some fifty to seventy-five yards, zigzagging while we ran, heading toward the hole in the wall from where Corser had called. Trautwein made it all right, and I almost did. Just as I started to go through the wall I guess I zigged when I should have zagged. A steel-jacketed rifle bullet cut through me without even the courtesy of slowing down, as if I were warm butter. It felt like a straight rod was shoved right through the middle of me, and I instantly thought I was killed. All of my clothes and my loose field jacket made it momentarily difficult to realize that the wound was just on the right side. The force of the bullet plus my forward momentum carried me beyond the wall and threw me flat on my face. For some reason, as I lay there, finally aware that I was still alive, I frantically reached for my first aid kit, as if I could have patched myself up.

I unsnapped the case and removed the small kit, but my nervous hand and arm sent it flying, and I couldn't find it. It was then I heard Ray Corser's voice calling from behind a house and saw him motioning for me to come on.

It has always griped me that I had to get shot while running away from the enemy, although I'll admit it's the direction I always liked best. Through the years, in the course of normal physical checkups, doctors have noticed the troughlike gouge running from my right breast to back under the armpit. They ask what caused it, and I say a German rifle bullet. They say "Oh!" assuming, I'm sure, that I was hit while charging the enemy, and I say nothing. I'm not about to tell them different.

The wounded and the few unscathed of the platoon were being collected in the basement of a house. The situation had degenerated to the

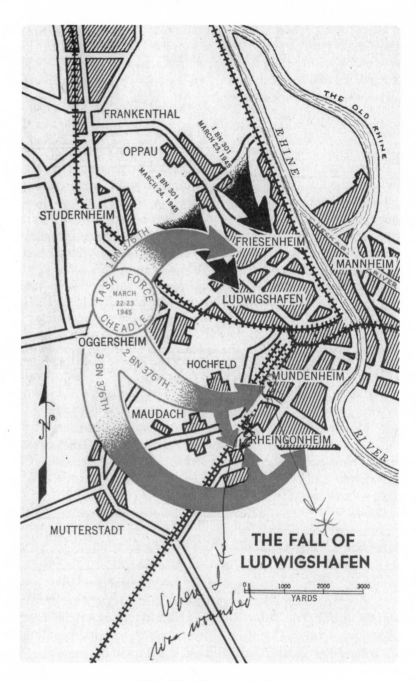

The fall of Ludwigshafen

point that anyone who could get off the field under his own power did so. I had no trouble walking, and as Corser led Trautwein and me into the house I could see the company commander directing the fire of one of our machine guns that had been set in one of the rear windows.

Once in the basement, I came under the attention of Dave Ray, the platoon medic. Ordinarily, he was a smiling, easygoing sort of fellow, but he sure had his work cut out for him that day. He had me strip to the waist, and there was a gaping hole in my right breast, with the bloody flesh protruding. I quickly turned my head after one glance. I hated the sight of anyone else's blood, and mine was even worse. Being young and dumb, as well as unable to see the hole of entry under my armpit, I somewhat got the impression that I had merely been hit by a grazing shot across the breast. If I had thought about it at all, I would have realized that even with zigzagging, it would have been impossible to have been clipped at such an angle, as we were basically running straight away from the line of fire.

Dave covered the wounded area with powdered sulfa, then he wrapped a big bandage completely around my chest. He had no sooner finished than screaming and running down the stairs came the young BAR man, Chuck Bray, shot in the groin. Dave immediately took care of him and gave him something for the pain. Next, the lieutenant came partway down the stairs, sat down dejectedly, and propped his carbine on one of the steps. He inquired as to who was still left on the field, and the platoon gave him the bad news. He said, "We've got to go out and get them!" I didn't hear any assent on the part of the able-bodied, and for once I didn't have to feel guilty. I had a great big gaping bloody hole in my chest, and was I happy—deliriously happy. I had a million-dollar wound that would give me a one-way ticket off the front line. This time it wasn't any frozen feet or a congested chest that no one could look at and really see anything. This time it was real flesh and blood, and was I glad!

After hearing no takers on his request to return to the fire-swept field, the lieutenant let the subject drop. It was one of those things that no one could really order anyone to do. Most of those left out there were probably corpses by now, and the cost of recovering the few others would likely be far too high.

The platoon sergeant, on hearing that I was wounded, stepped over and in a friendly manner told me to take it easy. You bet I was going to take it easy—easy back in a hospital. Part of me was stunned by the loss and wounding of my buddies, but another part of me was so elated over the prospect of getting away from this whole bloody mess that I could hardly contain myself. I had picked up a large cigar in a German house sometime back and saved it for a special occasion. I lit it up, figuring this was the time. There was a small wine cellar in the basement, the stubborn door of which I had to smash in with my boot. I retrieved a number of bottles and passed them out. I must have been some kind of sight sitting there with a big bandage over my chest, smoking a large cigar and drinking out of a bottle of wine.

It was a while before they could evacuate the wounded, so we had ample opportunity to sit around and talk. Since Ray Corser and Trautwein were the only two effectives left in the squad, we were commenting on how the squad had gone from twelve to two in just a matter of eight days: three on POW duty, three killed, and four wounded. Perhaps it was in the spirit of when one half of an elderly couple dies, and the other eventually has to smile and go on that caused Ray Corser's remark. With a big smile, he said, "Well, I guess that makes me squad leader!" And after a moment of hesitation, Trautwein, the veteran of one week, piped up with a big grin and said, "And that makes me assistant squad leader!"

For some mad reason, this reminds me of the old story about the horse race between the Russian horse and the American horse. The American horse won, and the Russian horse lost. The Russian newspapers truthfully reported that the Russian horse came in second and the American horse came in next to last.

Eventually the evacuation mill began to grind. Those of us who could walk were led and those who couldn't were carried by litter to the battalion aid. The general feeling was that those who made it alive to battalion aid had an excellent chance of surviving. It was located in a large room with benches around the walls in a building that might have once been an elementary school. The other companies had also had their share of problems, so the place was jam-packed with casualties either on the benches or on the floor. The majority of the soldiers looked like they were in a lot worse shape than I, so it was with great surprise that I heard the doctor, after examining me, turn around and say to the attendants, "Take this man out right away!" I couldn't see how a grazing shot could warrant so much attention.

My lot was merely to go along for the ride, however, which is what I did, literally. They made me lie down on a stretcher and immediately loaded me, along with some others, into an ambulance waiting out-side. I have no idea in which town the field hospital was located, but the trip was long enough to be out of German artillery range. Chuck Bray, who had been shot in the groin, had been placed in the litter above me. Evidently they had been unable to stop the bleeding, as all during the ambulance ride blood dripped on me from the canvas above. I wonder if he retained the camera with the film taken that next to last day.

The field hospital was in a huge institutional building of some sort with big rooms and long large halls. It must have served a number of divisions, as the floors of all the rooms and halls were littered with ca-sualties. I was supposed to lie on the floor and wait my turn for an op-eration, but I felt great, so I decided to explore the place. I ran into someone I knew who said he had seen my squad leader, Ben Siegel, and gave me somewhat general directions as to where I could find him. I finally found Ben after searching several rooms. He was lying on the floor, his head heavily bandaged from the bullets that had grazed him. He nodded that he knew me but couldn't talk. I wished him good luck and proceeded to return to my assigned area, stepping over soldiers all the way.

By now the right side of my chest had swelled up until it looked like I was trying to sneak out with a small watermelon tucked under my shirt. As I made my way through the halls, jibes were thrown at me from all directions. "Hi, half woman!" or "Hey, babe, come over here and lie down next to me!" or "Hey, doll, where'd you lose the other tit?" I merely returned a big grin or retorted that it had been shot off by the Germans.

The operating rooms were doing a booming business, the wounded like slabs of meat being run through on conveyor belts. Considering the time of night, the doctor/nurse team to which I was assigned might have been starting their thirtieth or fortieth operation. To save time I wasn't even given a general anesthetic, only a local. With great fear and trepidation I climbed up on the tall operating table, not hav-ing been cut on since my tonsils were removed when I was a child.

They had me lie on my left side near the edge of the table with my right arm extended backward. The table was at just the right height so that the nurse, who stood close, spent practically all the operation with her left breast jammed into my face or rubbing around on it. She was quite buxom, though not, of course, on a par with my watermelon. She was also quite attractive, but I don't remember the color of her hair, as I was preoccupied with other parts of her anatomy. A happening of this sort was beyond the pale of any former experience, so I was giving it all of my attention.

To add to the spirit of the occasion, the doctor and nurse, quite oblivious to my presence, were carrying on an interesting conversation about who was sleeping with whom these days. I have never decided whether the act on her part was completely unconscious or whether she was consciously adding her extra bit to the war effort to keep the boys' minds off their operations. For whatever reason, I can truthfully testify, with God as my witness, that I never gave the operation a second thought!

I don't know what they did, but I presume that along with other things they removed all the water from my wound, because when they were through, my chest was flat again.

Chapter Ten

The next stop was the huge permanent hospital at Verdun, France, on March 26. Though it was pure heaven to be in a clean bed with clean linens, for several days I went through withdrawal as if I were getting off drugs or alcohol. The effects of the past weeks came to bear, particularly those from the intense shelling at Lampaden. I felt like I was coming apart at the seams and my nervous system was starting to get away from me. I would tremble sometimes more than others. I hope I never again have to experience such feelings of helplessness.

I remember the dark-haired, slightly plump, warm and friendly nurse who took care of me. She appeared to be in her late twenties and was nice-looking and shapely. Since my needs at the moment were strictly for a mother figure it was in this manner that I viewed her, and I will always be appreciative of her attentiveness.

On March 28, I pulled myself together enough to write Mary Jo for the first time since I was wounded. Bitter memories of my last day at the front were still fresh in my mind. I wrote: "The 23rd of March was the worst day of my life. I mean our company got the living hell shot out of it. I was lucky to get out of it with only a flesh wound across the right breast. Most of my squad didn't get off so easy. There were only nine of us to begin with and three were killed, one was shot in a place where he will live but is ruined for the rest of his life, one got a hunk of shrapnel in his back, and my squad leader got two bullet wounds in the head. None of us were really more than kids—only one man in the squad was over nineteen. Jo, I've seen enough of this rotten, stinking mess to wish I was never born. However, I'm greatly cheered by the war news the last couple of days. Maybe the Germans will be licked before another month goes by.

"Right now I'm so far from the front it's pitiful. I'm in a very nice hospital in France living the life of Riley. I got here two days ago but didn't write because it was so nice to be in a bed again that I slept most of the time. No kidding, this hospital is really a vacation. They have a radio right outside my door that is hooked up to the Allied Expeditionary Forces program. It plays hot and swing music all day. What I like best of all is having my meals brought to me in bed."

Mary Jo's letter of March 17 went a long way toward lifting my spirits and putting some life into my veins. "Needless to say, I worry about you, but Dickie-boy, I know I'll see you again. That's one dream I know will come true. So often in my dreams you are stepping off a boat and I'm there, and the dream goes on from there. I wish I could put my head in your lap and go to sleep. It was so warm, and comfortable, and comforting. I love you dearly, Dickie-boy, and I miss you so much. It's a lot worse now than those months when we were apart before you went overseas. I didn't feel as close to you then as I do now. Now— well, all I can say is that if you were to walk in right now, and start to dance with me, I wouldn't dance a step. I'd just stand there and hold on to you."

I wrote her again on April 2, several days after my second operation. "You don't know what it means to be able to get cleaned up every day and sleep in a clean bed without fear of being awakened by one thing or another. In fact, I'm feeling like a human again and it really feels great.

"I was operated on for the second time last Thursday and got sewed up. I was doped to the gills when they took me to the operating room, then they gave me a shot of something in the arm and I woke up four hours later. I could have sworn someone was sitting on my chest trying to saw me in two with a ripsaw. However, I soon passed out again and slept another four hours. When I woke up the same guy was on my chest, but this time he was pouring hot soup on me. Fortunately as time went by the soup kept getting colder and colder and by Saturday I was merely stiff. By now it's not even very stiff and I'm not bothered at all if I don't get too frisky."

Later I wrote when I found out the true nature of my wound. "I got quite a surprise when I managed to peek under the bandage and found out that the gash across my breast (which I had thought to be a graze) was really where the bullet had come out and that I had never noticed the hole in my armpit. I thought I was getting a lot of undeserved attention! I was wondering why I was being x-rayed so much and every doctor I saw asked me if I could breathe all right and said I was mighty lucky. Evidently my lung had picked the proper time to take a siesta or something. Naturally the muscle along in there is pretty stiff but it is loosening up slowly but surely. The worst thing about it is that I'm afraid it will leave me with a couple of nice scars. This won't make any difference to you, will it, Jo? I guess I'll never be quite the bathing beauty I wasn't anyway, but I could have gotten off a heck of a lot worse."

Twelve days after I was wounded, on April 4, my parents received a telegram from the War Department. My parents had both been wonderful about writing me while I was in service. My father's answer to the telegram deeply touched me, and I will always treasure it. They, of course, had no idea of the extent of my injuries.

"My dear son, Richard: I just received a telegram, that most terrible event which I have always been hoping would never come! I received it at the office, and although Mother and I had decided that if one would ever come, we would wait and open it together, I see now that it is not possible to wait a moment. I opened it in almost a daze for fear of the worst. I know I turned white, and my hands trembled so I had to lay it down to see it, and all I could see was the words 'slightly wounded.' Thank God. Thank God a thousand times, it said 'slightly wounded!' Those words enabled me to rush upstairs to break the news gently to Mother. She met me at the door, but she saw the telegram I was trying to hide. She cried almost hysterically for just a moment, but because of the wording of the telegram she bore up magnificently and is phoning Mrs. Webster to see if it also read 'slightly wounded,' and Mrs. Webster says hers was worded the same, and he was so seriously wounded that we will be worried terribly until we hear from you. We will keep trying to find out the seriousness of the wound every way we can.

"We love you so much, Richard, and we are hoping and hoping. The news of your having been wounded will spread like wildfire. We will just have to tell them what we know without details. Alpha Bowman just came in and she broke down and cried, too.

"Do write us if you can, or have someone else write, and don't keep us in suspense. The worse the wound, possibly the worse for you, but to help compensate you can depend that Mother and Daddy will love you the more the worse the wound. Daddy."

The foxhole religion in which I had been baptized on the front line seemed to have a permanent quality to it this time. Considering the fizzles of my Rocky Mountain Spotted Fever and Bennett Spring State Park religious experiences, maybe the third time was a charm. It was finally getting through my thick skull that someone was trying to tell me something. Life, at best, was a process of standing with one foot on a banana peel, so I had better be prepared for the final slip.

My mother had given me a small New Testament, which I had always carried in my field jacket over my heart. I never read it but carried it as kind of a lucky charm. I particularly wanted it over my heart because I had read somewhere about a Bible deflecting a bullet. While in the hospital, however, I not only read the Bible, but I read it and read it! The net outcome of it all was focused on the fact that I felt called upon to share my enlightenment with others, especially in the area of their relations with women. I practiced this form of preaching for several months, as I would sit around with different groups of older men in the hospital, both in the replacement pools along the way to rejoining my outfit and also after joining them again in Wuppertal.

I was more or less tolerant of the ordinary run-of-the-mill unmarried fornicator who had no steady girl back home, but I came down hard on the ones who talked about cheating or wanting to cheat on their wives or sweethearts back in the States. I would show them Mary Jo's pictures and hold myself up as a shining puritanical example of faithfulness.

My stay in the hospital was quite pleasant. It included the watching of many movies and required only that I take part in the various exercise programs. While there I met and formed a friendship with a GI named Mike DeToma, who came from Louisville, Kentucky, which gave us something in common.

Passes to the town were difficult to secure, but Mike and I eventually got to do a little sightseeing around Verdun. While in town I took a picture in one of those "do it yourself" booths, and did I look emaciated! I had dropped from my fighting weight of 140 down to 118. As I look now at the picture of that skinny kid, how I'd love to share some of the 170 pounds I'm carrying around today.

For several days I shared a room with a personable chap about twenty-five years old. He would go into town during the day, and he looked very dapper in his uniform. At bedtime the first night I wondered what was going on when some nurses came in, and he patiently permitted them to place him into a straitjacket. I understood the reason later during the night, when nightmares caused him to repeatedly explode in a violent thrashing around on his bed.

The next day I questioned the nurse. She said that he had been with the Big Red One Division all the way through North Africa, Italy, France, and Germany. In the process he had been wounded six or seven times, but never seriously enough to be permanently removed from combat. It seems to me that after the third time, somehow from somewhere a voice should have cried out, "Enough is enough, send him home!"

I can attest to the urgency felt by the army to return the wounded to active duty. I had taken root in the comfortable surroundings of the large hospital complex in Verdun, and I would have been more than content to have remained there for the rest of the war. So you can imagine my shock and dismay when the doctor, after examining me, said that he was releasing me from the hospital. I said, "But Doc, I still have pus coming out of the corner of my wound." He responded, "Don't worry about it. It will be healed by the time you get back to the front." Yippee. Of course he had to be right. After passing through several time-consuming replacement pools, with medics checking on me along the way, by the time I reached my unit, I was healed.

I was discharged from the hospital on May 5 and was in a replacement depot near Thionville, France, when the war with Germany ended several days later. Everyone in the depot was happy, but there was little, if any, celebration. The possibility of being sent to the CBI (China, Burma, India) theater made the situation exactly the same as when we were back in the States in a port of embarkation sweating out going overseas.

On the 14th I was sent to a large replacement depot at Bonn, Germany; that day's trip was one of the most interesting that I ever experienced overseas. We drove in trucks through quite a bit of Belgium, the scenery being far prettier than anything I had ever seen in France or Germany. On the houses in practically all the towns and cities were hung the black, yellow, and red Belgium flag and usually the flags of the other Allies. Flowers covered the green rolling hills as far as you could see. Archways of flowers were also over the road in many places. The people were nicer looking and the houses much neater than in France.

I was especially glad to take this trip as it enabled me to see a lot of the cities that had undergone saturation bombing or been the scenes of heavy battles. We passed through Bastogne (where they stopped the Bulge), Houffalize, Duren, and Aachen. I could hardly believe such devastation was possible, even though my eyes were looking at it. Around Bastogne, where they had all the big tank battles, you could still see hundreds of German and American heavy tanks, light tanks, half-tracks, and so on littering the countryside.

During the war so much of the army's movement was done after dark for reasons of safety, I remember when we would sit down with our backs against a building, and tanks would pass by in ghostlike fashion, their cannons silhouetted against the night sky. Toward the last, when they started to get the huge Sherman tanks, their long 90mm cannons looked like naval guns.

When we were both stopped I was envious of tankers if they loaded souvenirs in their storage bins. There was precious little we could add to the one hundred pounds we were carrying.

As we went into Germany, all the way to Bonn, I was dismayed by the sight of devastation in all of the cities, similar to that in eastern Belgium. Men below the age of fifty were scarce, as most of them would be held in prisoner of war camps for some time.

There obviously was a tobacco shortage in Germany. We thought it funny to watch well-dressed Germans following GIs, waiting for them to throw away their cigarettes.

While in Bonn I made friends with a nice fellow in his thirties from Pittsburgh, Pennsylvania, by the name of Bob Pfeuffer. He had been in the printing business before entering the service. He was one of a number of persons with whom I foolishly thought I would faithfully maintain contact after becoming a civilian, but I never did.

By May 27 I finally joined up with my company once again and was surprised to learn of their travels since the day I had been wounded. All those weeks in the hospital I had been gloating over how much fighting I must be missing out on, with my company surely moving on east across the Rhine. As it turned out, the bums had only one more day on line after I left! Once Ludwigshafen had been cleared out, the Ninety-fourth Division was pulled back for a week's rest as Third Army reserve. Then the division was transferred from the Third to the Fifteenth Army, and took up positions on the west bank of the Rhine in northern Germany near Krefeld. The 301st and 302nd Regiments maintained tactical positions along the river, but their activity was limited to artillery fire and the frequent sending of patrols across the Rhine. The 376th, however, was placed in divisional reserve and given occupational duties near Willich.

With the German armies beginning to collapse and retreat a short time later, the 376th Regiment crossed over the Rhine to Wuppertal, and the balance of the division went to Dusseldorf, where occupational duties were performed. So it was a month later, on May 27, that I was joyfully greeted by Pat and other surviving members of the platoon, some of whom had just gotten back from the hospital themselves after being wounded at various times during the period the platoon was on line. The most common reasons for casualties were shrapnel, concussion from German artillery, and frozen feet.

I found out that Company E had been given an unusual assignment. We were detailed as a guard company for one of the Polizei Praesidiums, which in the heyday of Hitler's power had served as a Gestapo headquarters. Inside, as our charges, were 1,200 ex-Gestapo agents, SS troopers, and Nazi political leaders and diehards, who were awaiting final decisions on their possible indictment as war criminals.

The men of the company were billeted quite comfortably in surrounding houses, complete with all the facilities, including hot and not-so-cold running women for those who wanted them. Pat and I didn't want any, but if we had, most of the loose women had already been taken up, as the company had been there for a month. At the time I estimated that, of the attached men, about half were faithful to their wives and sweethearts back home and half were not. As I look at it now, this was really not too bad a percentage, considering the extreme situation of being thousands of miles away from home with temptation not only facing you but chasing you. At any rate, I perceived that I had ample fertile ground for my preaching on evil women and evil ways.

The prison itself was interesting. We had shifts eight hours out of twenty-four—four on and eight off, around the clock. The building had six floors, with two internal courtyards, and was capable of holding up to fifteen hundred prisoners. There were usually five guards to a floor, with one in the center and one sitting at each corner. Aside from checking on the prisoners, all we had to do was to see that they cleaned up their rooms and swept and mopped the halls in the morning.

By and large the prisoners were treated humanely, except that we would get a bit playful in our exercise programs. However, I did boot one guy in the rear for forgetting where he was and giving me a Nazi salute. Also, I'll never forget one GI who had backed an SS trooper into a corner and was driving a fist into his stomach. With every blow the trooper would give the stiff-arm salute and yell "Heil Hitler!" Among the twelve hundred prisoners were about fifty women, one of whom had killed nine GIs with poison.

The only clothes the prisoners had were those they came in with. They ate two meals a day, sometimes consisting of bread and coffee, and slept on beds that used boards for mattresses. Whenever a guard would enter a room, they would yell Achtung! (Attention!) and click their heels. In fact, all day long you would hear the steady clicking of heels resounding down through the halls. There were no latrines in the rooms, so they would come up before the nearest guard, stand at attention, click their heels, address you as "sir," and ask permission to obtain relief. On returning, they would go through the same procedure, asking for permission to return to their rooms.

The prisoners were supposed to get exercise, so when the officers or higher noncoms weren't around, we provided a variety. It certainly wasn't the type of punishment the war crimes trials would have meted out, but it sure was satisfying. For example, on one of the walls of the third or fourth floor was a huge mural that stretched for a great length. I guess it depicted the glory of industry, as it showed a horse pulling a cart out of a deep mine, with other carts standing on a small track, having already been pulled out. Strewn all over the surrounding ground in the mural were an abundance of large rocks. The idea of the special exercise was for one or two of the prisoners to hold the reins of the horse, others to help push the cart out of the hole, and most of them to simulate shoveling rocks into the carts that were topside.

It was the ordinary run of calisthenics, however, that brought out the drill sergeant in me. I merely passed on the little goodies my instructors had rammed down my throat in basic training, such as the "bear walk," the "kangaroo hop," and the "wheelbarrow." Taking about forty prisoners at a time, I'd have them go down to the end of the hall and come back, making sort of an elongated circle. Of course, the duck waddle was the best of all. There is where they would get down on their haunches, waddle, and "quack" at the tops of their voices. I'm ashamed to say it, but I could hardly stop laughing when those fat ex-big-shot Nazis would waddle down the hall yelling "Quack-quack-quack-quack!"

Some of the guard duty was outside in a tower with a mounted .30-caliber light machine gun and a spotlight. Most of it, however, was done inside, for which guards supposedly carried only clubs. Like some of the others I carried a pistol in a shoulder holster, carefully concealed under my field jacket. You didn't want any weapon showing, as some crackpot might conk you over the head, take your gun, and try to shoot his way out.

The pistol I was carrying was a brand-new sportsman-type Luger, taking a bottleneck bullet. The bullet had a 9mm base and a 7.32 point. Pat had bought it somewhere before I had rejoined the company, and I bought it from him. Of course, I paid a dear price for it, because friendship or no friendship, Pat was a shrewd businessman.

If the prisoners hadn't been probable war criminals I would have felt more sympathetic over their skimpy diet. Perhaps I looked to them like I had a kindly face, because on two occasions they came to me to present written petitions addressed to the "Kommandant." One of them came from a man who had been a big exporter, who had written several long pages. There was a man in the platoon who could read German, so I had it translated. He wanted permission to leave the city, go to his section of the country, get a load of food, and bring it back there to the kitchen of the prison. A mayor approached me with a similar petition the following day. I turned both petitions in to higher authorities, but I doubt if anything was ever done with them.

The building was a veritable paradise for exploration, so I took advantage of it. For one thing I was fascinated with the cleverly designed concrete guard boxes around the premises. I wondered if former Gestapo agents had lurked in them. The basement and subbasement were riddled with radio rooms and other rooms where the Gestapo no doubt interrogated and tortured their prisoners. I found much equipment and literature to inspect. I sent home several books showing beautiful colored pictures of various military organizations, along with some other literature and souvenirs. I had little competition, because I never saw anybody else down there.

Coming in the main entrance, you were presented with a huge staircase curving up to the second floor. It reminded me of those I had seen in movies that featured palaces and grand mansions. Along the staircase was a large marble balustrade that Pat and I both longed to slide down, like we had seen done in the movies. The first sergeant's desk was near the staircase, as you had to report to him before going on duty. One day as Pat and I walked in, we saw that the desk was vacant. Now was our chance. We bolted up the stairs to the second floor, jumped on the rail, and started sliding down the huge half circle until we landed on our rear ends on the marble floor below. After picking ourselves up, laughing all the while, we noticed the captain standing there, unsmiling, as if he failed completely to see the joy of it. He quietly asked us our names and platoon and went on his way. However, when we got off duty, the platoon sergeant called us on the carpet and issued some mild form of company punishment. I've forgotten what the punishment was, but whatever it was, it was worth it.

In addition to the staircase in the main foyer, there was also a statement by Adolf Hitler, emblazoned in bold letters in a prominent position on a wall, catching your eye as you walked in. Though I never thought much of anything else that Hitler said, this statement made a great impression on me, as it was the only German phrase that I ever committed to memory verbatim, and I retain it to this day. In German it read: "Eine volk das seine helden nicht ehrt, ist nicht wert helden gehabt zu haben." In English: "A people who do not honor their heroes are not worthy of heroes."

On learning of the translation, many times I would stand before the inscription and stare. All through my childhood fantasies of war I was always the hero, going far beyond the call of duty. It was I who drew my sword, pointed it toward the enemy, dug my spurs deep into the flanks of my steed, and led the charge of the Light Brigade. It was I who on countless occasions had led my troops over field, trench, and parapet. Why had real life been so different? Why couldn't I be the one who would try to inspire a rescue of Americans trapped in a pillbox? Why couldn't I be the one to run through shrapnel and bullets to drag a buddy over to the safety of a bomb crater? Why couldn't I be the one who would try to stir my platoon out of a basement into a fire-swept field to rescue the wounded? I couldn't because—it just wasn't me.

All the time I was overseas, Mary Jo was good about sending me food. The post office required the showing of a recent letter from a GI in which he requested food in order for them to approve the mailing. If I had failed to specifically mention food in my recent letters, she would write a fake letter as if it were from me to present to the post office. We saved a couple of those letters to herself "from me," and they're quite interesting.

Her first package sent to Wuppertal finally reached me. I wrote her, "That first box has really come in handy and I'm not kidding. The last four days when I came off guard at midnight, I've had a peanut butter and mayonnaise snack. Plus, of course, a bottle of beer. The company gets cases of the stuff from some brewery, using German marks. Just between you and me, I'd hate to have my fortune in those German marks. I haven't got it all figured out yet, but I think their currency is kinda screwed up."

We did have some free time to get out of the company area. One day Pat took me to meet a nice girl he somehow had become acquainted with prior to my returning to the outfit. She was stunningly beautiful, almost as if she could have been the homecoming queen at a football game. We stayed for only a few minutes at her parents' house, then went on to see Wuppertal's most outstanding attraction, which was the Schwebebahn.

The Schwebebahn was sort of a hanging trolley railway system, as far as I know the only one in the world. The car runs under the track instead of on top of it. Being supported only on one side, it has a tendency to sway. Running on electricity and traveling at a high rate of speed, it probably was capable of carrying seventy-five or more people at a time. The system covered about ten miles along and over the Wupper River, which twisted and turned around the Wuppertal metropolitan area, with platforms every three blocks to get off and on. With all the swaying as it traveled at a height of some fifty or sixty feet above the surface of the river, it was almost as much fun as an airplane ride.

Chapter Eleven

For several days there had been rumors that the Ninety-
fourth Division would be relieved by the British, and we would be
transferred to occupational duties in Czechoslovakia, leaving the Fifteenth Army and returning once again to the Third Army. The rumors
proved accurate, and on June 14 we moved out of Wuppertal.

The company that relieved us was part of the Seventy-first High-
land Light Brigade. However, only about 25 percent of them were Scottish, the rest being English. I found the Scottish brogue almost
impossible to understand; it sounded to me like someone talking with
mush in his mouth. The Scots all wore that flat cocked cap with a tas-
sel on it that I had seen in the movies.

After a short march we boarded boxcars that were forty feet by eight
feet; they put the whole battalion on the same train. The farewell scene
at Wuppertal, as the freight train started to pull out of town, made a
lasting impression on me. A number of women had come to say good-
bye and were standing at various boxcar doors all along the train. The
wailing and crying would have befitted a wake. I had previously assumed that all encounters were merely "playing around," but it
quickly became obvious to me, from the heartbreak I was witnessing,
that many genuine relationships had been formed.

Life seemed to have a way of going on, under whatever circumstances and in whatever location it was placed. These relationships
had little, if any, chance of continuing, as Czechoslovakia was a long
way off, and the United States, where we were to eventually return,

was a lot farther. Whether the women consciously admitted it or not, most of them must have realized that this was the final good-bye.

At this moment in history Germany was largely a nation of women; most of the men were either dead or in prisoner-of-war camps. I feel that my experience of seeing their grief, from a boxcar of a freight train slowly pulling away from the station, gave me an increased level of maturity. It also gave me an insight into how, down through the ages, there have often been marriages between men and women of different nationalities and races, whenever they have been thrown together. These German women were not crying because they were losing a food provider. They were crying because they were losing men they cared about.

Another thing came out of all of this, which I'm sure some of the older men deeply appreciated—I quit preaching to them.

The trip took about five days because the railways were still pretty banged up from the war. We had straw on the floor, which wasn't so bad for sleeping, but we would travel for fifteen minutes, then stop for two hours, travel for about fifteen minutes, then stop for another two hours.

The scenery was beautiful. Looking out at the rivers, plains, gentle hills, and mountains, as well as what seemed to be very good crops, I couldn't see why the Germans were always griping about not having enough room, because I sure was seeing a lot of space.

We finally arrived in western Czechoslovakia, detrained, and climbed into open-air trucks for the four-hour trip to the village of Razice, not too far from Strakonice. Our platoon and one other stayed here while the other two platoons of the company were assigned to another small village a mile or so away. We were to serve as a token force facing the Russians, who were located in other towns several miles to the east. We had heard the Russians were a pretty wild bunch, and we believed it that first night, when we heard them shooting off flares and tommy guns for amusement.

My squad and one other stayed in a sort of barn with a concrete floor, sleeping on straw we had brought in. During the day little kids would run in and out, speaking Czech, which sounded to us like ungodly jibberish. I managed to pick up a few words, but it was difficult. There was one little kid with whom I was waving the fat (I didn't know enough Czech to do any chewing), and I happened to find out he could play tic-tac-toe. Naturally, I defeated him with my superior tactics.

This small town of Razice had a town crier and a street cleaner who wore uniforms. There was a big bell that rang at 6 A.M., noon, 6 P.M., and 10 P.M., telling them the times to eat and go to bed. No good Czech was out after ten o'clock!

The people of the town were mostly what you would call peasants, going out in the daytime to work in their fields. They were friendly. The women were really rugged, and I would have hated to get into a fight with any of them. A lot of them would go barefooted into the fields and pitch hay onto the top of a high wagon all day long. I also saw many of them walking around with huge loads on their backs or sometimes on their heads. I felt like telling them the medieval days were over, but they'd probably have resented it.

One time I saw a flock of geese waddling by in formation; a mama goat followed them as if she were their shepherd. It was impossible to drive anywhere without honking the horn and trying to get the geese, ducks, and goats to move off the road. You'd see the Czechs using their cows to pull heavy wagons, and they even used dogs on occasion to pull lighter ones. Little lakes and ponds were everywhere. All in all it was a fairyland setting and left me with fond memories.

Our working hours were filled with the usual army routine of classes, marches, and tactics in the surrounding hills. In the many off hours, however, my correspondence with Mary Jo became frequent and lengthy, and we continued to grow closer to each other through our letters. The ardor of a youth deeply in love poured forth. On June 29 I wrote:

"Sweetheart, I love you. I guess you know that, don't you? More than anything else I want our love to last for a lifetime or perhaps forever. The last phrase was prompted by something of a religious feeling—a feeling that makes my heart skip a few beats when I think of my love for you never to end.

"It will soon be an anniversary for us—six months since the last time we were together. That's one night that is imprinted in my memory for keeps. With me that night were those beautiful blue eyes and cute little white hands that had long before attracted me. To say that this was all that attracted me that night would be very wrong. I guess what I'm really trying to say, darling, is that I love, cherish, and adore everything about you—all your ways, the pretty body that shelters them, yes, and even all your little faults. Jo, you're the only one for me. Of that there is absolutely no doubt in my mind and I'm merely living on the fact that I kinda think there is no doubt in your mind either. I love you, Jo Jo, with all my heart, Dickie."

My dad had written me after it was becoming obvious that Mary Jo and I were making subtle marriage plans, though not for the immediate future. Since we both played the piano, he wrote, "If you get Mary Jo I'll have to buy two pianos to start you out, I guess, so you can play at one end of the house and she at the other. On second thought I wouldn't have to get but one the first year, as you'd both probably want to sit on the same bench."

On July 10, I wrote Mary Jo, in reference to a letter I had just received from her, "Jo, honey, your whole letter was wonderful but your last paragraph affected me the most. At the time you wrote it you thought I was going straight to the Pacific. You said 'No matter how long you are away, I'll still be waiting.' I wish I could describe the feeling this gives me. It's like the time I was in the hospital and you wrote that you didn't care how badly I was wounded just so I came back to you alive. At the time you had no idea where or to what extent I had been injured. After reading that I nearly broke down, and if I had I wouldn't have been the least bit ashamed. Jo, darling, believe me, I'll love you with all my heart for the rest of my life just because you're you. But at the same time I'll always be indebted to you. Your GI (I love you) Jo, Dickie."

There were a lot of beautiful woods in the area that invited Pat and me to do a good deal of hiking in our free time. On several occasions we came upon small towns occupied by the Russians and stopped to chat with some of their sentries. Usually, at least one Russian in the group could speak German, and Pat would jabber away with his meager vocabulary. The Russians that we ran into surprised us by being so small. Most of them were smaller than me. They all had close haircuts and seemed friendly. However, compared to ours, their uniforms looked like rags, and their rifles didn't stack up to ours either. We'd swap rifles for a moment of friendly examination. Theirs were bolt operated, only holding a clip of four with one in the chamber, whereas our M1 Garands had a semiautomatic fire of eight. They were impressed.

Pat and I liked to walk, talk, and explore towns together, and many a friendly wrestling match took place on the concrete floor of that old barn. We formed that close kind of friendship that is possible only among the young, before maturity gets you so nitpicky on the personality of others. I'd talk about Mary Jo, and he would tell me about his girlfriends back home. We laid plans about the different businesses we would go into together after we got back to the States. I had no intention of going into the family business at the time.

Before we left Razice, the cigarette supply went from slow to almost nonexistent. I had quit smoking some time back, but whenever cigarettes were issued, smokers and nonsmokers alike received them. I usually held on to mine, and when the others ran out I could easily sell them. At this time, however, the price was skyrocketing because the supply just didn't come in. The price reached the unbelievable figure of five dollars a pack or fifty dollars a carton (about two hundred dollars a carton in today's currency). It's hard to imagine the nicotine habit being so strong. There must have been a general market value for them, as I was able to get a Czech woman to do a whole load of washing for two cigarettes.

On July 14 I received some of the best news I could have expected. I was being transferred to the headquarters battery of the Ninety-fourth Division artillery. For a few days we had been hearing rumors that some of the rifle companies' older combat veterans who had been wounded were being transferred to easier jobs. Though I was young, because of our high casualties, there were only a few who had been in combat longer than I. I had been hoping to get into a cannon or heavy weapons company or, if I was really lucky, a field artillery battalion. But I nearly passed out when I found I was going to be strictly rear echelon.

The division was still sweating out going to the Pacific to fight the Japs, so I was not the least bit heartbroken to be in a unit that had had only one casualty during the war, compared to three hundred fifty in our company, and the only reason he was wounded was that he went driving too near the front. This was my kind of outfit!

The battery had no field pieces of its own, its main job in combat being to handle communications between the firing batteries in the four field artillery battalions. I was assigned to a surveying section, but since those in charge were doing no tactical training I never did any surveying.

The town in which the headquarters battery was located had such a wicked name I can no longer remember it, and we soon moved to Volyne. Whatever the name was, it was in Sudetenland, about twenty or thirty miles north of Strakonice, and its population was practically all Sudeten German.

My biggest impression, however, was the feeling of going from poverty to luxury. During the war I always felt that the frontline units had received everything that was humanly possible to get to them, but now that the heat was off, it was a different story. Our little rifle company out in the hills had to sweat blood to get rations, salvage, equipment, and other supplies. For the last couple of weeks we had had the skimpiest of meals in our line and were really griping about it. Imagine my surprise to take my first feast with the new outfit in a beautiful hotel restaurant, being waited on by German waitresses. It was like going from a soup line to Antoine's in New Orleans.

Another thing I liked was the fact I only had to carry a carbine instead of an M1 rifle and could wear a pistol belt rather than a cartridge belt. The carbine seemed like a light toy after carrying the M1 for so long. Of course, there were some disadvantages, too. Being so near a lot of big brass you had to be a pretty-boy soldier—helmet liner varnished, ten-dollar fine for a pocket unbuttoned, and twenty dollars for not saluting, and so on.

After several days we moved out of Sudetenland to another town of about five thousand by the name of Volyne, some ten miles to the south of Strakonice. Our battery set up camp in a large, modernistic high school building on the edge of town. The men in the battery were a friendly bunch, and I liked them all, especially Phil Phares, my assistant section leader, and another man who was named Scott but called Scotty by everybody, of course.

Higher headquarters had called for a pretty tough schedule, but the battery commander, Captain Sears, was a good egg, substituting athletics for our regular daytime work. The battery was divided into four teams, playing softball for one half of the day and volleyball for the other half.

I would go swimming some in the evening in a pool they had in town. I'd had the town tailor make me a pair of trunks out of a towel. Unfortunately, they were too big around the waist, so it was unsafe to dive off the diving board. I used the one-armed sidestroke mostly.

There were also several pubs in town where I would go to drink a beer or two and visit with the people, who were friendly. Some who could speak English would express their fears about being taken over by the Russians. As it turned out, their fears were well founded.

There was usually opportunity to see three or four movies a week, of which I took advantage. The normal allotment of movies was one or two, but the boys who ran the special services for the division artillery were from our battery.

Table tennis was available at the enlisted men's club, and I played a great deal. It was the only sport at which I had ever been good. I had played it all through school and everywhere I could in the army, winning a championship in a small tournament put on by the hospital in Verdun. One night the ex-national table tennis champion of Czechoslovakia happened to be at our club, and I played him. He classed about fourteen notches above me, but it took him a little time to figure out my style. I won the first game before he came back and creamed me twenty-one to five in the second. Nevertheless, it has always been a point of pride with me to say I defeated the ex-national table tennis champion of Czechoslovakia in one game of table tennis.

Dances were held regularly, and they were attended by the local Czech girls, music frequently being provided by the division swing band. As a rule I would just go and watch. The Czech girls couldn't follow my style, and I'd be darned if I was going to do the polka! There were just two nights that were exceptions. On one night I found a dark-haired Czech with whom I could dance, and I walked her home afterward. As more or less a matter of form I kissed her goodnight—maybe twice. On one other night I danced with a slim "un-Czech"–looking blue-eyed blonde whom I also walked home. The next day one of the young men from the battery politely informed me that she was his girl and that he had just been unable to be at the dance that night. Since he was so gentlemanly about it all, I told him I would step aside. Besides, she hadn't let me kiss her goodnight.

These two incidents were innocent enough, and I was sure Mary Jo would have been broadminded and understanding. However, I didn't bother writing her about them. Other than this, I was a living perfection of behavior in Czechoslovakia.

I wrote my letters to Mary Jo while sitting at a desk that faced a window with a view of the whole valley. I could see Volyne and the hills beyond, which were studded with dark green forest and pretty fields. Considering all the recreational activities available, this had to be just about the best army life for which one could ever hope.

On August 3, I wrote Mary Jo that I was now an assistant jeep driver, and though I had to drive a lot of majors and colonels, it was sure great to get behind the wheel of a buggy again and go booting around the Czechoslovakian mountainside.

On one occasion I had to drive a youngish major back to the Sudetenland, in order to drop him off at the home of his girlfriend. On the return trip, well after dark, I entered a mountainous section filled with long curves. Sometime later, without warning, the headlights went out. I pulled to the side, stopped, and pondered. I figured it was a bad fuse, but I had no training as a jeep driver. I didn't know if or where a reserve fuse might be located or how to install one if I could find it.

A GI truck passed by at a fairly fast clip. Without thinking, I jumped on its tail and kept close to the taillights. This worked out well for a period. Then for some reason, perhaps because of inattention from stress or fatigue on my part, the truck was suddenly deep into a long curve off to my right. I should have stopped immediately and waited for daylight. With an overcast sky and without headlights, I could see absolutely nothing of the road ahead. All I had was a mentally envisioned estimated curved arc between me and the taillights.

I elected to go for it, reached the truck, and stayed close until we arrived at the next motor pool, where someone was good enough to fix the headlights, after which I continued my trip to Volyne.

Down through the years, at odd moments, I have pulled up this memory for review. Off to my far right I see a pair of taillights on a fast-moving truck. To my front I see complete blackness, which makes my skin crawl. I might use this episode as a prime example of eighteen-year-old poor judgment, except at the time of its happening I had already turned nineteen.

In another letter to Mary Jo during this time I told her about my mother's letter concerning Eisenhower's lifting of the nonfrat policy several weeks before. My thoughts stemmed at least in part from my experiences of life in Wuppertal as I wrote: "Mother wrote me July 17 and told me her disapproval of the lifting of non-fraternization, sending quite a few clippings, mostly involving the opinions of American girls. From several of her more recent letters I could gather she was wondering how her only child was behaving. I can't blame her, as I'd be the same way if a child of mine were so far away. At any rate, I put her straight. The non-frat policy had to be lifted. It was merely hindering men who could stay away from women, and those who couldn't (high officers, low officers, and enlisted men alike) didn't let any laws stop them. The law couldn't be enforced or 40% of the army would have been in jail. It's impossible for human laws to stop the desires of human nature, unless a man has religion or ideals. Jo, honey, these are two things you must believe of me. I have the faith of religion, if not the knowledge of all the technicalities, and certainly there's a lovely girl I still have to look square in the eyes. So-o-o goodnight darling, I love you very much, Dickie. P.S. Jo Jo, I love you."

On August 11 I wrote her about seeing Bob Hope's USO show at the Winterburg airstrip. I wasn't more than a hundred yards from the stand, but it was too far away to hear his natural voice, and the PA system was in sad condition. Nevertheless, I enjoyed him, Jerry Colonna, and the others very much.

The main topic of conversation in my letter, however, was the atomic bomb that had just been dropped on Japan. Though most of us in the battery had mixed feelings, it was hard not to be happy over not having to go to the Pacific theater.

"Jo, what do you think about this new atomic bomb? It, along with Russia's declaration of war, kinda spells 'fini' for the Japs. The war may be over now for all I know, as I haven't heard the latest news report. The Japs have offered to accept our terms if allowed to keep their Emperor. I imagine you feel like I do—you can't get very jubilant without thinking of what a terrifying and unbelievable thing this atomic bomb is. It's not hard to see that this old world is good for not more than one more war. Here's hoping mankind will harness this power only for peaceful and civilized advancement. Maybe I'm only asking for trouble to be thinking too much along these lines, because the end of the Jap war is nothing to be sneezed at. Gosh honey! Do you realize what all it will mean—I think I will immediately stop building up my hopes until I know for *sure* the war is over."

Our letters must have crossed midocean, because I soon received a letter from Mary Jo, and her reaction to the atomic bomb was quite different from mine. In part, she wrote, "When I got off work the newsboys were screaming, 'Extra! Extra! Read all about it! US drops atomic bomb on Japan, killing hundreds of thousands!' I bought a copy and read it on the bus going home. After reading several paragraphs, I started crying and didn't stop until I got home. It was so horrible. I couldn't imagine *my country* doing anything so terrible to innocent civilians. It's still a nightmare to me."

The next day was a big one for the Czechs in Volyne. They celebrated getting back a statue the Germans had taken from them. It was of a soldier carrying a wounded comrade. That night they built fires around the statue, and the Czech boys and girls put on a show. Ordinarily the people dressed in clothes similar to ours, but for the celebration many of them dressed in the old Bohemian costumes. All in all, it was quite colorful and sentimental.

Around ten days later, because of the Czech kids soon having to return to their school, our battery moved to the opposite side of town into what had been a small factory. A small river ran under part of the building, which presumably had been used to generate electricity. It was a nice setup with double bunk beds on both floors and German women to do our housekeeping. I had no sooner unpacked and settled in than who should walk in the door but Pat O'Connell with his big grin. He had come a good distance to visit me, catching a train from the company to Strakonice then hitchhiking the rest of the way. I showed him the sights of Volyne in the afternoon and took him to the enlisted men's club in the evening. It was good to hear the latest news from the company,

The next morning Pat and I thumbed our way to Winterburg, where Pat wanted to buy some material so that a tailor in Razice could make him a civilian suit. What a guy! I guess he wanted to mix with the people without their knowing he was an American soldier. We found the material he wanted but didn't have the ration slip needed to buy it. We tramped up to the office of civil affairs and tried to finagle the slip out of a captain; he explained that material could only be sold to Czechs as there was a big shortage. We finally gave up and hitched a ride back to the battery just in time to miss noon chow. I then found out I was on guard so Pat went back to the company, and I started saluting majors and colonels. Before we parted, I told Pat that now that I was a jeep driver I would figure out some way to get back to the company for a visit. I never managed it; events soon began to move too fast for me.

A few days later I bought a German burp gun from a man who had enough points to return to the States for discharge. Naturally he wasn't allowed to take it home with him. However, he had about three hundred rounds of ammo for it, so we hiked about a half mile out of town and proceeded to saw down a tree in one of the gulleys we found. It was a sweet-firing gun, and I enjoyed being on the nonbusiness end of it. The war was by now becoming far away to me, retreating into the dark recesses of my mind.

The dulling of memory with the passage of time, though we lose some good things, can be a blessing. How terrible it would be to always feel the fresh rawness of every pain. Just several days before, I had written Mary Jo some of my reflections on the war. I continued on by saying, "Jo Jo, when I think back on it I've got about a thousand and one experiences that a person doesn't normally go through. The funny part about it is that it's hard for me to realize that it was actually me who went through them. Not that all of them were so horrible but that they were so strange to anything I had ever done before or after."

On September 6 I was informed that another man from the battery, Ralph Brunn, and I would be given three-day passes to Paris. He also had been transferred from my old rifle company to the battery. We excitedly made preparations and left on the train from Pilsen on the 8th, arriving in Paris three days later. We stayed in one of the many hotels taken over by the Red Cross. The rooms were nice, and the food was excellent, plus it was served by cute French waitresses.

During the three days we covered all the main tourist attractions, such as the Palace of Versailles, the Arc de Triomphe, the Cathedral of Notre Dame, and the Louvre. Ralph had a camera and got shots of everything, including each of us lying in a stone Egyptian bathtub at the Louvre when the guard wasn't looking. I would have loved to have had these pictures, because even if I had the chance in the future, when would I ever again have the nerve to get into an Egyptian bathtub in a museum? Unfortunately, there wasn't time for me later to get copies of these shots from Ralph, and when we started keeping in touch after we got home, he had misplaced the pictures. The shops were interesting to browse through, and we bought a number of small gift items, among them what was to be Mary Jo's first bottle of Chanel No. 5.

We were fascinated by the street cafés and enjoyed sipping glasses of wine at a little round table and watching all the women parade up and down the sidewalk. They really knew how to dress and wore funny hairdos and hats. I estimated that about 50 percent of them dyed their hair; some of them even used a purple color.

The *pissoirs*, public urinals, were something else. They were really public. Even at the busiest intersections, a metal shield rarely covered more than the buttocks, leaving the legs, shoulders, and head exposed to the view of all the women passing by. I'd be darned if I was going to use one of them.

I've told about the days, but the nights were another story. You remember that I said I was a living perfection of behavior while in Czechoslovakia. It was true, but I didn't say anything about Paris! I was repeatedly telling Mary Jo in my letters of the maturity I had now attained, but Paris proved that there was still a good deal of the ornery boy left in me.

During the first day I ran into Delbert Dougan, a high school friend of mine who had been in the Franklin Club, and we made plans to get together that evening. That night Ralph Brunn and I joined Delbert and his two buddies for a little celebration. Like us, they were on three-day passes. We decided to go first class and go to the night club that was located part way up on the Eiffel Tower. Once there, we ordered five quarts of champagne, one for each of us, and watched the floor show. I had done no drinking in quantity since the poker parties prior to going into service. Since then my drinking had rarely consisted of more than one or two beers or a small amount of wine at any one time.

But this was Paris, and we were all in the mood to celebrate. It was my first champagne, and it tasted great. It was cold and slid down easily. I can't vouch for the others, but I polished off my quart to the very last drop. I recall going up the Eiffel Tower, but I don't remember going down. Judging by the way I felt, I could have easily floated down.

At any rate, Ralph went on to a USO show, and the rest of us began to walk the streets of Paris. I was in high gear, and as far as I was concerned, Paris was mine, and I was going to enjoy it.

Of course, we weren't the only ones walking the streets of Paris. When the sun went down the streetwalkers came out in droves. I can truthfully say I was never tempted in the least. The movies they had shown us in basic training had done their job well, and when the women approached they merely conjured up an image of a mass of dripping VD. However, this did not prevent me, especially in my present drunken state, from showing off to my peers and having some fun.

You must remember this was long before movies like *Klute* or *Pretty Woman* and the many articles on the rights of prostitutes, showing the basic truth that they were still human beings with their own personalities and feelings. I am ashamed to admit I merely looked on them as fair game and as objects with which to make sport.

They would usually approach in small groups, indicating they were available for hire. I would show an interest, picking out the most voluptuous of the group, and though the "Charmin test" had not yet been invented, I would proceed to test out her breasts, one with each hand. I figured that through the clothing there was no possible way I could be contaminated. The squeezing, I think, was reminiscent of the squeezing done to the large rubber bulbs to honk the horns of the old touring cars.

I was continually amazed at how they would stand so patiently, motionless like a cellophane-wrapped piece of meat at the market, which you would poke with your fingers, trying to decide whether or not to buy. After a few "honks," a big grin would come over my face, and I'd say, "Sorry, no good!" Next would follow a long, loud stream of invective, hurled by the group in my direction. I didn't know any French, but it wasn't hard to get the drift. This anticipated response, of course, merely added to the spirit of the occasion.

After "honking" several groups, I began to tire. The champagne was wearing off, and I was running out of steam. I must emphasize that it was I alone who engaged in these barbaric practices. But the others did watch and laugh.

As I collapsed onto my bed back at the hotel, I dutifully took out my wallet, flipping it open, as always, to Mary Jo's picture. However, upon casting a bleary eye on her image for only a split second, I slammed the wallet shut. After all, Paris at night was no place for the eyes of a girl like Mary Jo!

The second night in Paris was on a much higher plane. I attended the USO dance and hit it off very well with a sweet young French girl with light brown hair. She was the daughter of a French diplomat, spoke perfect English, and lived with her parents on the other side of the city. I wanted to escort her home from the dance, but it was impossible to do so by public conveyance as she had ridden her bicycle. Therefore we walked clear across the city of Paris, talking and pushing her bike. With gendarmes waving us through intersections, the walk across Paris at night was a memorable experience for a young man. Arriving at her home, I kissed her goodnight—maybe twice.

I confess I was smitten—perhaps influenced by the balmy September night and the light fragrance of her hair. We agreed to meet again at the dance the next night, my last, where I planned to write down her address. She never arrived. I wondered why.

In 1996 Mary Jo and I celebrated our fiftieth anniversary by taking a trip to England and France. We crossed the Atlantic Ocean at night in a British airliner. The lights were turned low in the cabin, but I was awake in my aisle seat with Mary Jo sleeping soundly beside me.

I stopped a steward and told him that my eighth-generation ancestor, Henry Kingsbury, had come from Assington, population three hundred, just a short distance north of London. At age fifteen he had sailed with Governor Winthrop's fleet to Massachusetts in the year 1630. He surprised me by saying his wife had come from Assington and they were going to build a house there in the very near future.

A population of three hundred against England's population of thirty million made this mathematically one chance out of a hundred thousand. Could this be a night of magical coincidences? I suspected such because when we were boarding, a group of French teenage girls moved into seats a short distance in front of us. Their leader was a small, nice-looking woman about my age, who spoke perfect English to the stewards. I had an odd feeling that I had seen her before. Could this be the girl with whom I had walked across Paris?

With Mary Jo sleeping, I thought of walking to the front. The French-woman was in about the fifth seat over in the middle section. The French teenage girls were still awake, giggling and laughing. In my fantasy, I asked "Pardon me, are you the leader of this group? . . . Yes, I am. Are they disturbing you? . . . Absolutely not. It's just that you seem familiar to me. By chance did you happen to live in Paris shortly after the end of World War II? . . . Yes, I did. I've lived in Paris all my life. . . . Did you ever attend the GI dances sponsored by the American Red Cross? . . . Yes, I went to them regularly. . . . Was your father a French diplomat? . . . How could you possibly know that? . . . Do you remember dancing the entire evening with a young GI, when you were supposed to be sharing your dances with others; and after the dance he walked you and your bicycle all the way across Paris to your home? . . . Yes! Yes! . . . Would you please step to the back—Why didn't you come to the dance the next night? . . . I had stayed out so late, my mother wouldn't let me go." At this point in my imaginary encounter, Mary Jo materialized in the aisle beside me. "Introduce me to your friend, Richard." Pop! End of fantasy.

However, the magic held on through the small hours, and by the time we landed in London, I had definitely decided upon my plan of action. As soon as we disembarked, I would go up to her and ask her if she was the girl I had met in Paris. Unfortunately, by the time we got off the plane, the group of teenage girls and their leader had scurried far ahead.

It probably wasn't her anyway. Or was it?

Chapter Twelve

On returning to Czechoslovakia I was transferred to the or-
derly room as assistant battery clerk. I guess the fact that my records
showed one year of typing in high school got me the job. Unfortunately, I had never practiced since school and was doing good to type
twenty words a minute, mostly with the two-finger method. To make
matters worse, I'd turn a sickly green every time the lieutenant would
give me a division or division artillery report to type up and say, "Rush
it." The nice thing about the job, however, was it gave me a promotion
to corporal.

One day I was writing a letter to Mary Jo when I was interrupted by
some news that seemed like a miracle. I continued with my letter. "Jo,
honey, I feel kinda funny. I'm shaking like a leaf. We received orders to
move out early tomorrow morning for Klatovy, which isn't very far
from here. But that isn't a hundredth of it. The Colonel called down and
said there was one vacancy for a thirty day *furlough to the United States,*
providing that man wasn't more than thirty years old and had less than
thirty points. Because most of the men in this battery are original men
there's only one person eligible—*me.* Oh golly, I can't think straight!"

The idea was that the furloughs would be given to men who had
nine months or more remaining of their two-year service and would
return to Europe after the furloughs were completed. I never had to return; I finished my tour of duty stateside at Camp Polk, Louisiana.

The suddenness of this unexpected move caused a thought to pop
into my head, and I wrote Mary Jo: "The only thing that is really im-

perative is *please* don't throw my letters away. This may seem like a funny thing to say now, but if I don't say it now I may be too late to stop you. It's not that you'd hurt my feelings, honey, but I'm trying to think of the future. Don't you see, we have the story of a good part of our life in letters. I've saved all of yours and someday we'll be able to pair them off (well, four of yours to one of mine) and enjoy what we said in answer to what."

My orders came through a few days after the battery moved to the city of Klatovy, and I was on my way back home. Scotty drove me to the railway station, and as we parted he stuck out his hand and said, "It's been nice knowing you." For some reason these words became indelibly imprinted on my memory. There were hundreds of other partings as I moved from unit to unit during the time I was in the army, but they were always on the basis of "I'll be seeing you," as if in some strange way we would surely run into each other again. Reunions, of course, never took place in a vast country the size of the United States, where you lose contact with old school friends, even though they live in the same metropolitan area. It was Scotty and Scotty alone who seemed to grasp the fundamental truth that whatever there was to friendship it was now locked and sealed, never to grow or expand or escape, except in memory. He wrapped up whatever value there was with his words, "It's been nice knowing you."

At the railway station I joined with a small group from other units of the division, all of us returning to the States. The others were Bob Kwantz, Ray Gai, Carl McKellips, and Ed Farris. Farris was in command, as he was a sergeant, but it was with Ray Gai that I struck up a friendship. He had been a water bill collector in San Francisco.

It was a long trip by train to the port of Marseilles in southern France, after which we were stuck in a staging area for an additional two weeks waiting for shipping orders. Ray and I got only one pass to the seaport, but I made use of it to sell on the black market an extra pair of combat boots I had. The grapevine told us where to go, and I remember a shady character leading us up to a second-floor room in which were lurking some of the roughest, toughest-looking pirates I had ever seen. Having my Luger under my jacket made me feel safe and secure. As I look back on it now, I realize that if they had wanted to, that bunch of cutthroats could have sliced us into little pieces before I could have gotten my Luger halfway out of the holster. Fortunately, I completed the transaction, and we went on our way.

The combat boots were the only thing I ever took from the army, and someday my conscience may cause me to reimburse them. However, great difficulties are presented when I think of their value now with compound interest!

My orders called for me to go straight to Jefferson Barracks in Missouri to be released for my furlough. Mary Jo had arranged with her boss to get two weeks off work, planning to spend one in Kansas City and the other with me when I came to Louisville. Since the depth of our relationship had grown mostly through letters, the thought of being with her face to face brought with it some apprehension. I wondered if she loved me as much as I loved her. I wrote from the staging area, "As soon as I get to New York, honey, I'll try to phone you. And if my voice seems cracked, it won't be because I'm getting old—it'll be because I'm scared!"

When Mary Jo heard from me of the strong possibility of my return home some six months early, she wrote:

"You know how it is with bubbles—they are lovely, but if you touch them they burst. Well, I'm half afraid that if I think too much about your last letter—the one saying you're coming home—I'll get a letter tomorrow saying it isn't really going to happen. I have dreamed of that happening so often, but now that there is a possibility it seems too good to be true. Oh, honey, if it could only happen. You'd be surprised if you could know how excited I feel inside at the prospect of seeing you again. It's as though some little gremlin is in the pit of my stomach twirling an egg beater. Everyone I know has their fingers crossed for you, Dickie-boy, and me—well, I crossed my heart, my eyes, and if you'd teach me the art of crossing toes I'd try that, too."

In response to my request to save my old letters, she wrote: "Incidentally, I won't throw your letters away, although they are spilling out of every drawer in the house—some are boxed. I didn't want to; all I needed was your masterful command to keep them and I got it. Oh, Dickie, I do love you so very, very much. All my love, Mary Jo."

We finally received our orders to board a ship. With great regret I disposed of my burp gun, falling victim to the army's constant warning that all duffel bags would be carefully searched before boarding, and anyone found with automatic weapons would lose his opportunity to return home. As it turned out it was all a big bluff. I could have brought home all the kaiser's crown jewels, as I never saw them search anyone's bags. I sure would have liked to have that schmeisser as a souvenir, but I just didn't dare take a chance on not getting to return home.

We boarded a small slow-moving Liberty ship and headed southwest along the coast of Spain. The Mediterranean Sea was a beautiful dark blue, as still and quiet as a small lake. Just before we came to the Strait of Gibraltar they issued everyone some goodies, including a can of Planter's peanuts. Not having had any peanuts since coming overseas, I proceeded to polish off the whole can. We then passed through a very visible line where the color of the water changed suddenly from a dark blue to an angry green. The waves of the turbulent Atlantic began to toss the little Liberty ship up and down, and the peanuts in my stomach went right along with it. I hadn't been bothered with seasickness on the trip over on the huge luxury ship *Ile de France,* but this was a different story. I became so sick I was afraid that I was going to die and then afraid that I wasn't. It was almost twenty years before I could once again look a peanut in the face.

I have lost all records and memory of the exact date our ship arrived in New York harbor, but it was sometime toward the tenth of November 1945. As I had left the United States from Boston, this was my very first sight of the Statue of Liberty. As it came into view a wave of excitement swept the ship. I wished Pat could have been with me.

As young people often do, we both failed to clearly get the other's home address. He had forgotten what city I lived in, but I knew he was from Green Bay, Wisconsin. However, by the time I called directory information in Green Bay, he had evidently moved out of the city, as there was no Patrick H. O'Connell listed. Just on a hunch, I would call Green Bay every few years to see if he had moved back. Finally, in 1969 information had him listed. I called immediately, and he thought it was a ghost from the past. We made arrangements, and Mary Jo and I visited him, his wife, Jay, and his three sons for a three-day period that following summer.

It was quite a reunion, reliving the old times. It was funny that though we shared many common memories, we each had our own individual memories of the things that had been vivid to us. Later, through letters, I tried to talk Pat into bringing his family down to Kansas City for a summer visit. It all became academic, however, as he had an unexpected brain hemorrhage; and like the suddenness of a screaming 88mm shell that carries off a friend, when the dust had settled, Pat was gone. With whom shall I now talk about the war?

But all this was in the future as we approached the old lady holding her torch on high, along with sixty-one years of the happiest married life that any man ever had the right to expect.

At that moment Ray Gai and I were happy—deliriously happy—as was everyone else, jumping all over one another like schoolboys.

The war was really over. And we were home.

A Historical Note

The Role of the Eighteen-Year-Old Replacement

——————— Though I had learned a great deal about eighteen-year-old replacements from personal observation, in recent times I wanted to learn more. I called the Library of Congress, and the reference librarians there steered me to the purchase of one of those books that nobody except military historians reads: *The Procurement and Training of Ground Combat Troops in World War II.*

The eighteen-year-old replacements received little or no recognition because they were never a separate unit; they never trained with the units in which they fought, but as individuals they were dropped in pots of hot boiling water.

The year was 1944. The draft age had been lowered to eighteen, but neither Congress nor the general public wanted the draftees to enter combat until they turned nineteen. As low-risk rear-echelon and support positions had long since been filled, eighteen-year-old draftees were sent to Infantry Replacement Training Centers (IRTCs) set up all across the nation.

Smaller numbers were sent to Armored Replacement Training Centers (ARTCs). After graduating from seventeen-week basic training they were placed in various kinds of temporary duty. Thousands were placed in special nondivisional regiments, and many more were assigned to newly formed advanced infantry replacement training centers. Here they were held until they were nineteen, at which time they would be ushered into the overseas replacement pipeline.

Additional thousands were sent into fourteen infantry and three armored divisions on the East Coast. These divisions were tied up and prevented from being deployed overseas because they had eighteen-year-olds within their ranks.

Upon reading this, I was struck by the most unusual situation. On one hand, the tying up of seventeen divisions, along with the various holding facilities, appeared to me logistically unsound. On the other hand, the U.S. Army was demonstrating a surprisingly compassionate attempt to bend over backward to comply with the wishes of the general public and Congress to not send eighteen-year-olds into overseas combat.

Unfortunately, after we suffered huge losses at the start of the Battle of the Bulge in late December 1944, eighteen-year-olds were no longer a protected species. The supply of eighteen-year-olds pouring out from the infantry training centers continued until the end of the war in an ever-increasing flow, due to a lowering of physical requirements and a reduction of allocation to other theaters of operation.

If not for the large infusion of eighteen-year-old replacements from January 1945 to the end of the war, the frontline units of the divisions in Europe would have been badly depleted, resulting in a tremendous loss of effectiveness from shrinkage and consolidation. By the end of the war in May 1945, these frontline units were largely made up of eighteen-year-old replacements.

In Stephen Ambrose's book *Citizen Soldiers,* he tells of the many 1944 high school graduates who were replacements and were attaining a high level of combat effectiveness after a few days on line. His book also shows charts of the forty-three infantry and fifteen armored divisions in Germany, along with the percentage of losses.

In many divisions these losses ran 200 percent or more. To understand losses of this magnitude, I think it best to picture frontline units such as rifle companies, platoons, and squads, as frameworks with revolving doors. Casualties are constantly leaving, while replacements and recovered casualties are returning. In my rifle squad we would start out with twelve, but in roughly two weeks we would be down to about six. Then they would fill us back up to twelve.

There was no hint in the congressional material of the depth of depletion of the training centers by the Battle of the Bulge. I discovered this after writing an article about eighteen-year-old replacements that was published in the *Kansas City Star.* I then sent a version of the article to the Ninety-fourth Infantry Division quarterly publication, which goes all over the country. I had always griped about being pulled out of basic training with only fifteen weeks of my seventeen-week training, because I missed the part about how to operate satchel and beehive charges. My heart had stopped when someone from supply dropped one of each in my foxhole when we faced a large number of pillboxes at Wiltingen.

In response to the quarterly publication I had many contacts from former eighteen-year-old replacements who had also had their training cut short—some to twelve weeks, some to ten weeks, and some to as little as eight weeks. I heard the worst case recently from my high school friend Dean Stringer, whom I had run into by chance on the boat going overseas. He had received only six weeks' training at the armored replacement center at Camp Hood, Texas. He may have told me of his six weeks' training on one of the nights we looked at the Atlantic Ocean over the guardrail of the *Ile de France,* but who can remember details of every conversation held sixty-two years ago?

In any event, I was sent to the Ninety-fourth Infantry Division, and he was sent to the Eleventh Armored Division, where they placed him in a tank. There was just one little problem. He hadn't reached the part of training where they teach you how to fire the cannon. So they rushed him out back and gave him a crash course on how to fire a tank cannon. Dean's tank was later knocked out, and he spent a year at a hospital in Denver, Colorado, recovering from head wounds.

In World War II the armed forces of the United States at their peak numbered approximately 12,350,000. The army's share of this total was roughly 8,300,000. An exact figure for the eighteen-year-old replacements would be irretrievable, since they were sent in all directions to overseas combat openings. However, judging from totals of training center graduations, which were made up of mostly eighteen-year-olds at the time, plus the various storages, I would estimate their total to be far in excess of 300,000.

It was the older men, because of their maturity and experience, who were largely the recipients of those medals given for acts of valor. Few eighteen-year-old replacements probably ever advanced above the rank of private first class during the war, as their time in battle was short. Yet, as individuals, they filled the battle-vacated slots in the frontline units of the fifty-eight American divisions in Germany plus those divisions in Italy under General Mark Clark, allowing these frontline units to remain viable.

It is for this reason I feel recognition of their service is long overdue.